1-4-99

Check Out Receipt

Henderson County Public Library
270-826-3712
www.hcpl.org

Monday, Aug 4 2014 11:26AM
STAUFFER, JACOB

Item: 33009000972218
Title: Readings on A separate peace
Call no.: 813.54 Read
Material: Book
Due: 08/25/2014

Renew items online, by phone, or in person.
Overdue & reserved items cannot be renewed.
Fines on videos & DVDs are $1.00 per day. Fines
on books, audio tapes, & CDs are $0.10 per day.

READINGS ON

A SEPARATE PEACE

Other Titles in the Greenhaven Press Literary Companion Series:

THE GREENHAVEN PRESS
Literary Companion
TO AMERICAN LITERATURE

READINGS ON

A SEPARATE PEACE

Jill Karson, *Book Editor*

David L. Bender, *Publisher*
Bruno Leone, *Executive Editor*
Bonnie Szumski, *Series Editor*

Greenhaven Press, Inc., San Diego, CA

Every effort has been made to trace the owners of copy-righted material. The articles in this volume may have been edited for content, length, and/or reading level. The titles have been changed to enhance the editorial purpose. Those interested in locating the original source will find the complete citation on the first page of each article.

Library of Congress Cataloging-in-Publication Data

Readings on A separate peace / Jill Karson, book editor.
    p.   cm. — (The Greenhaven Press literary companion to American literature)
    Includes bibliographical references and index.
    ISBN 1-56510-826-4 (pbk. : alk. paper). —
ISBN 1-56510-827-2 (lib. : alk. paper)
    1. Knowles, John, 1926–   Separate peace.
I. Karson, Jill. II. Series.
PS3561.N68S437   1999
813'.54—dc21   98-35701
                                            CIP

Cover photo: Photofest

Copyright ©1999 by Greenhaven Press, Inc.
PO Box 289009
San Diego, CA 92198-9009
Printed in the U.S.A.

66It seemed clear that wars were
not made by generations and
their special stupidities, but
that wars were made instead
by something ignorant in the
human heart. **99**

—*John Knowles,* A Separate Peace

Contents

Chapter 1: Symbols in *A Separate Peace*

A Separate Peace takes place at the Devon School, which is recognizable as Knowles's alma mater, the Phillips Exeter Academy. Nora's study of both Exeter and the fictional setting reveals how Knowles departed from reality in his creation of the highly symbolic Devon landscape.

Three sets of symbols structure *A Separate Peace:* the summer and winter terms, the Devon and Naguamsett Rivers, and peace and war.

The novel's two main characters are schoolboys named Gene Forrester and Phineas. Bryant elucidates why these names are highly descriptive and shows how they function on a symbolic level.

Chapter 2: Technique in *A Separate Peace*

The first sentence of *A Separate Peace* establishes that the story is reverting to the past. This return to the past means that the narrator—separated from the events and their retelling by fifteen years—is able to accurately interpret events for the reader.

Knowles infuses *A Separate Peace* with opposing elements, such as the peace of prep school life and World War II and Gene and Finny's contrasting views of life. The novel's counterpoint develops and supports the story's basic theme, the loss of innocence and growth to maturity.

A Separate Peace is narrated by two Gene Forresters: Young Gene effectively conveys the feelings and vitality of the immediate scene while an older—and wiser—Gene provides the reader with reliable commentary.

Chapter 3: Important Themes in *A Separate Peace*

Chapter 4: Characterization in *A Separate Peace*

and ineffectual. Knowles's derogatory treatment of adult characters leaves the novel bereft of suitable role models.

FOREWORD

*"'Tis the good reader that
makes the good book."*

Ralph Waldo Emerson

The story's bare facts are simple: The captain, an old and scarred seafarer, walks with a peg leg made of whale ivory. He relentlessly drives his crew to hunt the world's oceans for the great white whale that crippled him. After a long search, the ship encounters the whale and a fierce battle ensues. Finally the captain drives his harpoon into the whale, but the harpoon line catches the captain about the neck and drags him to his death.

A simple story, a straightforward plot—yet, since the 1851 publication of Herman Melville's *Moby-Dick*, readers and critics have found many meanings in the struggle between Captain Ahab and the whale. To some, the novel is a cautionary tale that depicts how Ahab's obsession with revenge leads to his insanity and death. Others believe that the whale represents the unknowable secrets of the universe and that Ahab is a tragic hero who dares to challenge fate by attempting to discover this knowledge. Perhaps Melville intended Ahab as a criticism of Americans' tendency to become involved in well-intentioned but irrational causes. Or did Melville model Ahab after himself, letting his fictional character express his anger at what he perceived as a cruel and distant god?

Although literary critics disagree over the meaning of *Moby-Dick*, readers do not need to choose one particular interpretation in order to gain an understanding of Melville's novel. Instead, by examining various analyses, they can gain numerous insights into the issues that lie under the surface of the basic plot. Studying the writings of literary critics can also aid readers in making their own assessments of *Moby-Dick* and other literary works and in developing analytical thinking skills.

The Greenhaven Literary Companion Series was created with these goals in mind. Designed for young adults, this unique anthology series provides an engaging and comprehensive introduction to literary analysis and criticism. The essays included in the Literary Companion Series are chosen for their accessibility to a young adult audience and are expertly edited in consideration of both the reading and comprehension levels of this audience. In addition, each essay is introduced by a concise summation that presents the contributing writer's main themes and insights. Every anthology in the Literary Companion Series contains a varied selection of critical essays that cover a wide time span and express diverse views. Wherever possible, primary sources are represented through excerpts from authors' notebooks, letters, and journals and through contemporary criticism.

Each title in the Literary Companion Series pays careful consideration to the historical context of the particular author or literary work. In-depth biographies and detailed chronologies reveal important aspects of authors' lives and emphasize the historical events and social milieu that influenced their writings. To facilitate further research, every anthology includes primary and secondary source bibliographies of articles and/or books selected for their suitability for young adults. These engaging features make the Greenhaven Literary Companion series ideal for introducing students to literary analysis in the classroom or as a library resource for young adults researching the world's great authors and literature.

Exceptional in its focus on young adults, the Greenhaven Literary Companion Series strives to present literary criticism in a compelling and accessible format. Every title in the series is intended to spark readers' interest in leading American and world authors, to help them broaden their understanding of literature, and to encourage them to formulate their own analyses of the literary works that they read. It is the editors' hope that young adult readers will find these anthologies to be true companions in their study of literature.

INTRODUCTION

Gene Forrester, the narrator of *A Separate Peace*, observes early in the novel that "nothing endures, not a tree, not love, not even a death by violence." Indeed, *A Separate Peace* is a novel about change, specifically the change from adolescence to adulthood, of learning from experience, of moving beyond the loss of innocence.

The story unfolds against the distant trumpets of World War II. Yet Knowles is not as concerned about the harsh realities of this global conflict; the battles in *A Separate Peace* are fought not on the battlefields but in the heart and soul of the prep school student Gene, who struggles to come to terms with his enmity for his best friend, Finny. Gene's personal war and subsequent "peace," however, are not confined to the prep school life so eloquently described in *A Separate Peace*. Rather, Knowles uses the relationship between Gene and Finny, a friendship undergirded with envy and rivalry, to explore deeper psychological truths that are both timeless and universal. Readers from different generations and backgrounds will surely recognize Gene's psychological struggles, his fall from innocence, and his need to be absolved from guilt.

A Separate Peace is outwardly simple and so short that it can be read in a single sitting. In addition, the theme of man in conflict with himself is not new—it has dominated all types of literature. Yet Knowles's prose is so polished, his creation of atmosphere so precise, and his handling of plot and character so masterful that *A Separate Peace* will surely endure as a deeply satisfying work of fiction.

To aid the reader of this highly acclaimed work, *Readings on* A Separate Peace provides fifteen comprehensive essays to guide analysis and interpretation. The critical selections are divided into four groupings. To facilitate study of the work, each critical essay includes an introduction that summarizes the author's main idea. A biography and chronology not only provide important information about John Knowles but also highlight the historical events that influenced the creation of *A Separate Peace.* Other features include an annotated table of contents, a thorough index, and a bibliography for further research.

Few critics would disagree that *A Separate Peace* is a thoroughly engrossing story. Using *Readings on* A Separate Peace as a tool, readers are invited to move beyond the immediate story line and formulate their own analysis of this rich and multifaceted work.

JOHN KNOWLES: A BIOGRAPHY

The publication of *A Separate Peace* made John Knowles an instant well-known figure in the literary scene. Twenty-five years later the author commented:

> When my publishers told me in 1960 that they were going to bring out my first novel, *A Separate Peace*, on February twenty-ninth, I should have suspected that something unusual was going to happen. The book would appear on Leap Year Day, a date occurring only once every four years, a day created to set the calendars, and by extension, the cosmos, to rights, an omen day.[1]

By all accounts the publication did mark the beginning of events that—especially for a previously unknown author—were quite unusual: The slim volume that Knowles once predicted would sell only three thousand copies has since sold over 9 million copies, received rave reviews and prestigious awards, been adopted as curriculum by high schools and colleges across the country, and provided Knowles with an annuity for life.

CRITICAL RECEPTION

A Separate Peace has received almost unequivocal praise. Critics have called the novel "a gem of controlled eloquence," "a model of restraint, deeply felt and beautifully written," and even "artistry of a high order." The most unusual feature of commentary on *A Separate Peace* is the apparent lack of discord among critics. While they may disagree on particulars of the book—the significance of different motifs, for example—few would challenge the novel's status as a literary classic worthy of continued attention.

With such a critical reception, Knowles's name, it seems, will remain forever linked with *A Separate Peace*. True, Knowles continued his writing career after *A Separate Peace* made him famous, publishing ten additional books to date. All, however, met with cooler receptions than did *A Separate Peace*. With mixed critical reviews, not one has even remotely approached the critical acclaim of *A Separate Peace*.

What, then, accounts for the stellar success of Knowles's first novel? Part of the appeal of *A Separate Peace* is Knowles's talent for evocative atmosphere and imagery. Too, the novel's adolescent relationships bear a ring of authenticity. Knowles describes a setting and events that, to some degree, he experienced firsthand. *A Separate Peace* follows a group of students at a New England preparatory school during the early years of World War II, and Knowles himself attended a prep school during the war years. The story of John Knowles's early life and the creation of *A Separate Peace* are inextricably entwined, as Knowles once wrote: "What I set out to do in the novel was to unscramble, plumb, and explain what had happened during a very peculiar summer at Phillips Exeter Academy in New Hampshire, where I was a sixteen-year-old summer-session student in 1943."[2]

KNOWLES'S EARLY LIFE

John Knowles was born and raised in Fairmont, West Virginia, a small town with a population of about twenty-nine thousand. Born September 16, 1926, he was the third child of James Myron and Mary Beatrice Shea Knowles. Many residents of Fairmont were in the coal business, and James Knowles was no exception; the elder Knowles was vice president of the Consolidation Coal Company.

The young Knowles attended public school through the ninth grade in Fairmont. John's older brother had attended Mercersburg, a preparatory school in Pennsylvania. The Knowleses expected their youngest son to follow in his brother's footsteps. One day, however, John found a catalog from Phillips Exeter Academy—a New Hampshire prep school with which he was quite unfamiliar—lying around the house. On an impulse he described years later as "just for the hell of it," Knowles filled out the application and mailed it in. Thus, the chain of events that would ultimately result in Knowles's creation of *A Separate Peace*, and worldwide fame for its author, had been set in motion.

EXETER

While World War II raged in Europe and Asia, and scores of U.S. servicemen were journeying to war theaters overseas, Knowles had more immediate concerns: entrance exams required by Exeter. His performance was less than stellar, although his essay on the novel *Jane Eyre*, written as part of the exam, showed promise. Test scores notwithstanding, he was admitted to Phillips Exeter Academy in September 1942, although he was put back a year.

Exeter was academically competitive and rigorous; at first, Knowles feared he would fail. Within a short time, however, he honed his study skills, immersed himself in his schoolwork, and discovered his untapped potential. Studying diligently, Knowles was passing every course with ease by the end of his first term.

Knowles the student enjoyed Latin, French, and other languages. He also recognized the high quality of the education he was receiving, commenting that "the best teaching I ever experienced was at Exeter."[3] One faculty member, in fact, left a particularly enduring impression on Knowles, who wrote:

> I took both Latin I and Latin II with Mr. Galbraith. A finer, more inspiring teacher I never encountered. By the time he was through with me, I thoroughly understood the nature and structure of a language, and he had crucially influenced both my thinking and the way I expressed it in words. I am the writer I am because of him.[4]

In addition to his studies, Knowles befriended classmates who would later serve as models for characters in *A Separate Peace*. He based the character Phineas, for example, on his friend and fellow student David Hackett. Like Phineas, Hackett excelled in athletics.

In the novel, Phineas is tragically injured after forming the Super Suicide Society, whose members jump from lofty tree branches into the river below. Unlike his fictional counterpart, Hackett was never crippled by a fall from a tree, although students of the 1943 summer session did form a club whose members jumped from trees into rivers. Rather, Knowles transformed a rather benign accident to himself—he injured his foot after a bad fall from a tree—into the tragic maiming of the unforgettable Phineas.

The character of Brinker in *A Separate Peace* is modeled after another classmate with whom Knowles came in contact his first year at Exeter: Gore Vidal. Gore was a senior when Knowles entered Exeter and the two became good friends only after they had graduated from Exeter. Yet Gore piqued the curiosity of Knowles, who observed the older student from afar and later used his impressions to create the character Brinker. After the novel's publication, Knowles commented on his friend's connection to a character who, albeit interesting, is endowed with somewhat less than perfect attributes. "I haven't seen Gore since I told the world that he was Brinker. He will be flattered. Anyone is flattered to be used as a model in a book. If you paint the most terrible, villainous portrait of them, they are still secretly pleased that you found them interesting enough to put them in a book."[5]

LIFE DURING WAR

Satisfying educational endeavors and friendships aside, the war exerted its influence on the small New England prep school campus. Like the rest of the country, students at Exeter had to adapt to the unusual circumstances dictated by war. As one faculty member commented in the *Exeter Bulletin* in 1942: "One would be far astray to conclude that the Academy is untouched and unmoved, or unwilling to be moved, by the war. For over a year the same winds that have been blowing through the outside world have swept through the school, leaving many changes behind them."[6]

For one, the war created gaps in faculty positions. Following the Japanese bombing of Pearl Harbor in December 1941, most of Exeter's younger teachers were required to serve in the military, leaving teaching positions open. To alleviate this situation, class size—usually limited to a dozen or so students—was increased. Substitute teachers, unfamiliar with the school's tradition, were brought in. Whether substitute or regular, however, the faculty consisted of teachers who were too old for war duty, usually well over fifty years old. These factors created somewhat of a chasm between the students and faculty, leaving students with few companions or role models. Knowles recalled of the 1943 fall term: "I remember how virtually all the younger masters disappeared one by one, and old men became our only teachers. Too old to be in any way companions to us, they forced the class of 1943 to be reliant very much on itself, isolated. Maybe that made us stronger in a certain way."[7]

Knowles's alienation from the faculty is clearly reflected in *A Separate Peace*, which features primarily old and ineffectual teachers. Commenting on how his own experiences shaped *A Separate Peace*, Knowles reflected, "[The faculty] just were too old, too tired, and too busy. One of the reasons that Gene and Finny develop this intensely close friendship is that they had no one to relate to; no older person to pattern themselves on, to look at and talk things over with, they only had each other."[8]

Though the war left the school bereft of younger teachers, it simultaneously created a more tolerant faculty and generally more permissive atmosphere at the school. Probably reflecting Knowles's own experience, Gene in *A Separate Peace* comments:

> I think we reminded them of what peace was like, we boys of sixteen. . . . We were careless and wild, and I suppose we could be thought of as a sign of the life the war was being fought to preserve. Anyway, they were more indulgent toward us than at any other time. . . . We reminded them of what peace was like, of lives which were not bound up with destruction.[9]

THE ANTICIPATORY PROGRAM

Many Exeter students would reach the age of eighteen—draft age—before graduation. Thus, the Anticipatory Program was born. Designed to allow boys to graduate before they were eligible for the draft, the Anticipatory Program, through special summer sessions, accelerated the normal academic program. In addition, the War Department recommended that courses in this special program concentrate on mathematics, physics, English, and history, classes that would benefit young men entering the armed services. In short, the Anticipatory Program made students work harder.

Knowles himself attended the Anticipatory Program in the summer of 1943, partly because he had been put back a year and needed to catch up on his academic requirements. Despite the war and its attendant hardships, however, the summer term proved idyllic. By this time, Knowles had not only overcome any academic limitations, but also harbored a growing fondness for Exeter. Years after he wrote *A Separate Peace*, Knowles recalled:

> It was that summer that I realized I had fallen in love with Exeter. . . . The great trees, the thick clinging ivy, the expanses of playing fields, the winding black-water river, the pure air all began to sort of intoxicate me. Classroom windows were open; the aroma of flowers and shrubbery floated in. We were in shirt sleeves; the masters were relaxed. Studies now were easy for me. The summer of 1943 at Exeter was as happy a time as I ever had in my life."[10]

Although Knowles remembers these years as happy, he and other students had to adjust to the myriad inconveniences caused by war. Gasoline rationing and tire shortages, for example, curtailed automobile travel, resulting in less travel to and from school and also less frequent visits from parents. Because so many people were forced to rely on public transportation, trains were crowded and behind schedule, making trips home for the holidays difficult. Food too was limited; Exeter students subsisted on meatless meals and treats like candy became a luxury. Perhaps even more acutely felt, the defense industry started to draw on the female labor supply, leaving Exeter bereft of maid service. Students were forced to perform their own domestic chores, an unusual situation in an exclusive boys' prep school during the 1940s.

Throughout this time, Knowles and other Exeter students did what they could to contribute to the war effort. In addition to raising money for war bonds, students volunteered in community services "for the war." Many helped to harvest apple crops. Others shoveled snow from the railways to keep the lines open. Some students even donated their blood, weekly, to Exeter's infirmary.

THE PSYCHOLOGICAL TOLL OF WAR

Faculty changes, accelerated academics, and the physical hardships attached to those emergency years were indeed keenly felt by Knowles and his fellow classmen. Yet more pressing, however, was surely the psychological toll on students who, with military service imminent, would soon be headed for the battlefields. In *A Separate Peace*, Knowles plumbs the depth of the war's effects on soon-to-be-combatants. Perhaps mirroring Knowles's own preoccupation with the war while at Exeter, Gene Forrester says early in *A Separate Peace:*

> Everyone has a moment in history which belongs particularly to him. It is the moment when his emotions achieve their most powerful sway over him, and afterward when you say to this person "the world today" or "life" or "reality" he will assume that you mean this moment, even if it is fifty years past. The world, through his unleashed emotions, imprinted itself upon him, and he carries the stamp of that passing moment forever.
>
> For me, this moment—four years is a moment in history—was the war. The war was and is reality for me. I still instinctively live and think in its atmosphere. These are some of its characteristics: Franklin Delano Roosevelt is the President of the United States, and he always has been. The other two eternal world leaders are Winston Churchill and Josef Stalin. America is not, never has been and never will be what the songs and poems call it, a land of plenty. Nylon, meat, gasoline, and steel are rare. There are too many jobs and not enough workers. Money is easy to earn but rather hard to spend, because there isn't very much to buy. Trains are always late and always crowded with "servicemen." The war will always be fought very far from America and it will never end. Nothing in America stands still for very long, including the people, who are always either leaving or on leave. . . .

It is this special America, a very untypical one I guess, an un-familiar transitional blur in the memories of most people, which is the real America for me.[11]

CALL TO ARMS

By 1943, the army, navy, air force, and marines were drafting civilians to boost the Allied manpower. Exeter was not unaf-fected; over 3,000 Exeter men were called to service, and of these, 154 were killed.

In 1944, Knowles again attended the Anticipatory Program, completing several courses that enabled him to graduate early. He enrolled at Yale in the fall of 1944 and finished his first term before going into the air force. Knowles never saw the battle-field, however. As part of the aviation cadet program, he spent his time in training programs in Texas and Illinois. Knowles was discharged from service shortly after Japan's surrender in August 1945 brought the war to a close. Military duty fulfilled, Knowles was free to pursue his education.

Back at Yale, Knowles's writing talent began to show itself. He set his sights on an English degree. In addition to his class work, he contributed stories to the college magazine *Yale Record*. Another Yale publication, the *Daily News*, employed Knowles as a "heeler," a job that required proofreading and other light editorial skills. Ultimately, Knowles worked his way up the editorial ladder to become editorial secretary of the publication. Perhaps even more telling of his literary abil-ities, Knowles presented an entire novel as his senior essay.

Despite these successes at Yale, however, and in spite of the school's lofty academic reputation, Knowles's college ex-periences fell short of Exeter. Years later, Knowles compared the two schools, describing Exeter's pivotal role in his career:

> Yale was a distinct let-down [after Exeter]. The teachers there either read their year-in-year-out lectures to us in large audi-toriums, or, meeting us in small groups, seemed preoccupied with their extramural careers or reputations or whatever. They did not seem to be there primarily for us. It was Exeter which taught me how to approach new material, organize it, and express it.[12]

Misgivings aside, Knowles graduated from Yale in 1949 with a bachelor's degree.

PURSUING A WRITING CAREER

Soon after his graduation, Knowles obtained a job as a re-porter with the *Hartford Courant*. Two years into the job, in

1952, he quit so that he could travel through England, Italy, and France. While abroad, he wrote the novel, *Descent to Proselito*. Although it was initially accepted for publication, the book never made it into print. Novelist Thornton Wilder, who read the unpublished manuscript, offered Knowles the following advice: "Everything in this novel lacks intensity. . . . Find a subject which you are deeply moved about, very much absorbed in. . . . Select your next subject from the compelling elements in your life. It is from our most vital subjectivity that we write." [15] Wilder's advice had a profound impact on the young writer. Years later, as he started the novel that would become *A Separate Peace*, Knowles did indeed find a subject that, in Wilder's words, "deeply moved" him.

Following the disappointing outcome of his first novel, Knowles returned to the United States, moved to New York, and set out to make a living as a freelance writer. During this time, he published several nonfiction articles in *Holiday* magazine. In 1953, *Story* magazine published Knowles's first story, "A Turn in the Sun." Three years later, *Cosmopolitan* magazine published "Phineas," a short story that contained material that Knowles would develop in *A Separate Peace*. In 1956, Knowles moved to Philadelphia to take a position as an associate editor for *Holiday*. He would stay with *Holiday* for four years, contributing articles on varying subjects.

A SEPARATE PEACE

In 1954, at the age of twenty-eight, Knowles started work on *A Separate Peace*. Even though he was still on the editorial staff of *Holiday* and could not devote his full attention to the novel, the writing came easy for him. Describing how the book was written, Knowles claimed:

> *A Separate Peace* wrote itself. No book can have been easier to get down on paper. What was required was to be home in bed by midnight, get up at a quarter to seven in the morning, throw some cold water at my face, drink a glass of orange juice and a cup of coffee, and then sit down at my desk and take up my pen. Five or six hundred words later, written in an hour, I would get up and go to work as the editor of a magazine. [14]

Although he did not think the book would ever have a wide audience—he was once quoted as saying, "Who's going to want to read about a bunch of prep schoolboys and what happened to them long ago in the past?"—he did believe that the book was worthy of publication. He sent the manuscript to a literary agent who in turn submitted it to eleven of the nation's most prestigious publishers. It was rejected by every one of them.

Knowles's fortunes soon changed, however. A London firm, Secker and Warburg, showed interest in the novel and shortly thereafter, in 1959, published the British edition of *A Separate Peace*. The British critics' response was extraordinary; without exception, every reviewer praised the novel. Not surprisingly, American publishers vied for the rights to such a well-received novel. On February 29, 1960, Macmillan published the first American edition of *A Separate Peace*.

CRITICAL RECEPTION IN THE STATES

Paralleling the British reaction to Knowles's first novel, the response of the American literary press was overwhelmingly positive. The *New York Tribune* called the novel an "admirable exercise in the craft of fiction—disciplined, precise, witty, and completely conscious of intention." In a similar vein, the *San Francisco Chronicle* called it a "book that has great depth of meaning which should be read by every person who likes to think about a book after reading it." The *New York Times* concluded that Knowles was a writer "skilled in craft and discerning in his perceptions."

To Knowles's satisfaction, seven thousand copies were sold in that first printing. Soon after, the book went into its first paperback printing. Knowles was pleased, feeling that the book received the attention it deserved. Yet he never fathomed the extent to which the public would embrace his first novel. Recalling events years later, Knowles observed, "It was as though a wave, a very large wave, was gathering force, and moving toward me. There was a far-off rumbling coming nearer." [15]

A LITERARY LEGACY

Indeed, *A Separate Peace* acquired, in Knowles's own words, a "destiny apart" from his own. Despite his early predictions for the novel and its rather humble beginnings, *A Separate Peace* did not sink into obscurity after its early printings. In 1960 it won both the Rosenthal Award from the National Institute for Arts and Letters and also the William Faulkner Award. Meanwhile, sales of the book climbed steadily. With a rapidly growing audience, Knowles was deluged with letters from readers praising the book. Thousands of teachers found the book worthy of academic study and began adopting it for classroom use, a practice that continues in high schools and colleges today. Perhaps most indicative of the novel's continuing appeal, *A Separate Peace* has gone through over seventy printings, sold over 9 million copies, and continues to sell about five hundred thousand copies a year.

With royalties pouring in from the sales of *A Separate Peace,* Knowles was free to devote his full attention to writing. In 1960, he resigned from his job at *Holiday.* Soon after, he traveled overseas, visiting many countries in Europe and the Middle East. His experiences abroad would provide a wealth of material for future books.

KNOWLES'S LITERARY CAREER

In 1962, Knowles published *Morning in Antibes,* a novel based on his experiences on the Riviera. Two years later, he published *Double Vision: American Thoughts Abroad,* a series of essays based on his travels to the Middle East. The novel *Indian Summer,* published in 1966, became a Literary Guild selection. The story follows a wealthy Irish American family in Connecticut. In 1968, *Phineas: Six Stories,* a collection of short stories, was published. Another novel, *The Paragon,* which examines undergraduate life at Yale, followed in 1971. The following year, Hollywood released a movie adaptation of *A Separate Peace,* which was filmed at Exeter. The novel *Vein of Riches,* a historical novel centering on the coal industry, was published in 1978. Knowles also wrote a sequel to *A Separate Peace,* titled *Peace Breaks Out,* published in 1981. Like its predecessor, *Peace Breaks Out* is set at a preparatory school, but features different characters. *The Private Life of Axie Reed,* a novel set in Greece, was published in 1986. Several of these books were moderately successful, but none has approached the critical acclaim of Knowles's first novel. Indeed, it would be difficult—even for a writer as accomplished as Knowles—to equal the stature of *A Separate Peace.* While its ongoing sales figures are testament to the novel's permanence in the literary world, on a deeper level, readers of all ages and demographics continue to be drawn to this beautiful and profoundly meaningful story. Perhaps Knowles himself best sums up why *A Separate Peace* continues to move generation after generation of readers:

> *A Separate Peace* is one long and abject confession, a mea culpa, a tale of crime—if a crime had been committed—and of no punishment, or only interior punishment. It is a story of growth through tragedy. Young people, on their deepest emotional level, respond to that. It makes not the slightest difference that the story's externals may be totally foreign to them.

In the novel there is not a girl in sight; that means nothing—women of all ages and every background treat it as central to their view of life. It takes place among some privileged kids in a first-class preparatory school: that doesn't mean anything either. One of the most moving letters I ever got was from the teenage participants in a drug treatment program in the Bedford-Stuyvesant section of Brooklyn. Another was from a group of paraplegic veterans of the Vietnam War. Co-eds in Finland, old ladies in Italy, a murderer on death row in Utah—all have communicated their depth of feeling about the book. . . . The ultimate importance of *A Separate Peace* is that it has reached out to the readers who need it.[16]

John Knowles resides in Fort Lauderdale, Florida.

NOTES

1. John Knowles, "My Separate Peace," *Esquire*, March 1985, p. 106.
2. Knowles, "My Separate Peace," p. 108.
3. John Knowles, "A Special Time, A Special School," *The Exeter Bulletin*, Summer 1995, from http://www.exeter.edu/library1/separate_peace/article2.html, p. 1.
4. Knowles, "A Special Time, A Special School," p. 2.
5. John Knowles, "On *A Separate Peace*," *The Exonian*, November 1, 1972, p. 2.
6. M.R. Williams, "The Academy in Wartime," *The Exeter Bulletin*, July 1942, from http://www.exeter.edu/library1/separate_peace/war.html, p. 2.
7. Knowles, "A Special Time, A Special School," p. 1.
8. Knowles, "On *A Separate Peace*," p. 2.
9. John Knowles, *A Separate Peace*, New York: Bantam Books, 1959, pp. 16–17.
10. Knowles, "A Special Time, A Special School," p. 1.
11. Knowles, *A Separate Peace*, pp. 32–33.
12. Knowles, "A Special Time, A Special School," p. 1.
13. Knowles, "My Separate Peace," p. 109.
14. Knowles, "My Separate Peace," p. 106.
15. Knowles, "My Separate Peace," p. 108.
16. Knowles, "My Separate Peace," p. 109.

CHAPTER 1

Symbols in *A Separate Peace*

Symbolic Landscape

Sister M. Nora

The story of *A Separate Peace* takes place entirely at the Devon School, a New England prep school for boys. This setting is based on fact as much as fiction; according to John Knowles, Devon is actually the Phillips Exeter Academy, the school he himself attended as a youth. In the following reading, Sister M. Nora compares the actual and fictional school settings and concludes that Knowles augmented, suppressed, and exaggerated the physical features of Exeter. By taking artistic license, Nora contends, Knowles made Devon a rich, symbolic landscape, a setting capable of supporting such a meaningful story. Nora contributed the following essay to *Discourse.*

When Gene Forrester, in the opening scene of John Knowles' novel *A Separate Peace*, returns to the Devon School in New Hampshire fifteen years after his graduation, the landscape he encounters is immediately recognizable, almost to minute detail, as that of the famous boy's prep school, Knowles' *alma mater*, The Phillips Exeter Academy, Exeter, New Hampshire. In a letter to Mr. William J. Cox, Secretary to the Academy, dated December 14, 1959, Knowles wrote, "The setting on [sic] the novel is Exeter Academy, although I have called it 'Devon' for the usual reasons. The book is fiction and it is not a *roman a clef,* but I believe it would greatly interest people who know Exeter." But art does not use reality exactly as it is, or was, and a careful study of both the school in the novel and The Phillips Exeter Academy seems to reveal that the actual buildings, playing fields, and rivers have undergone an artistic process that combines elimination with heightening, during which they have suffered "a sea change / Into something rich and strange" —the symbolic, interior landscape of the Devon School.

Reprinted from Sister M. Nora, "A Comparison of Actual and Symbolic Landscape in *A Separate Peace,*" *Discourse*, vol. 11, 1968, by permission of Concordia College, Moorhead, Minnesota. Endnotes in the original have been omitted here.

TRANSFORMING EXETER

Gene says at the beginning of the novel, "There were a couple of places now which I wanted to see. Both were fearful sites, and that was why I wanted to see them." The first is The First Academy Building. Knowles uses it here in the opening scene, and later in much more detail as setting for the "inquiry" into Finny's fall, almost exactly as it still appears to the visitor today. In Latin, over the main entrance, there is the inscription, *Here Boys Come to be Made Men.* The foyer, the marble staircase branching left and right, the two left turns to enter the Assembly Room with its black Early American benches and raised platform, are all there in reality and in the novel. In the portrait of "a young hero now anonymous who looked theatrical in the First World War uniform in which he had died," Knowles has made a minor and unimportant omission, perhaps because he did not want to be specific about an actual person. Ensign Stephen Potter '15, who died in 1918, is fully identified on a plaque below his portrait. It reads, "First American Naval Aviator to bring down a German Plane in the World War. He lost his life in combat against seven enemy planes, April 28, 1918."

Knowles effects only one bit of very significant transformation of the realities of The First Academy Building. He gives both the Assembly Room and the foyer below it polished marble floors. Only the staircase is in reality marble. The foyer has always been finished with black and white blocks of rubber tile. The floor of the Assembly Room, also, has never been marble. Originally of small mahogany blocks, it was later changed to asphalt tile. By eliminating these more prosaic floors and heightening the hard, cold marble effect of his setting, Knowles the artist is translating mere realistic details into the language of symbol. He emphasizes that marble floors elsewhere in the school are treacherously dangerous for Finny when his leg is encased in a heavy cast. The marble staircase of The First Academy Building will break his leg a second time as he rushes headlong from the moment of truth that comes with Brinker Hadley's investigation. It is appropriate that the floor of the trial room should be marble also. Marble is Finny's enemy physically; it is also his enemy symbolically because it comes to mean that "something ignorant in the human heart" which kills Finny and makes wars.

Knowles again uses this technique of omitting what does not serve his artistic purpose and augmenting what is useful to it, when Gene, his protagonist, arrives at the second place he has come to see. This is the tree from which Finny, founder of the Super Suicide Society of the Summer Session of 1942, suffers his ultimately fatal fall. Fifteen years after the incident, Gene, taller, successful, more secure, finds that the tree which "had loomed in my memory as a huge lone spike dominating the riverbank, forbidding as an artillery piece, high as the beanstalk," is only one of "a scattered grove of trees, none of them of any particular grandeur." Here Knowles is being almost scrupulously true to the facts that Gene would have found on returning to the Academy in, as the book indicates, 1957 or 1958. There are today many trees along the bank of the river that Knowles calls the Devon, which could be the tree of *A Separate Peace.* Several could qualify for age and size and even for limbs extending over the river. None can be identified by the "certain small scars rising along its trunk" which make Gene certain that he has found it. This is not because Knowles' jumping tree is purely fictional. Like almost all his other details of setting, it is, or was, real. Miss Wendy French, assistant at the Davis Library of The Phillips Exeter Academy, says that the tree of the novel was known to most Exeter youngsters during her childhood because they often swung out on a rope from its extending limb and jumped into the river which really is deep enough for diving. Like many other trees along the river bank, very much like it in appearance, the tree was cut down in the summer of 1963 or 1964 because it had Dutch elm disease.

The one fact about the tree that Knowles suppresses in his story is that, according to Miss French, it was about four feet to the right of a small concrete bridge which still crosses the river and which is labeled, "The Hill Bridge 1914" and "Gift of A Member of the Class of 1865." Knowles, it seems, did not report the presence of this bridge because it would only weaken the mood of secrecy and isolation that the Spur Suicide Society needs for its illicit pranks. Instead Knowles concentrates on the all-important tree and exaggerates its size, color, shape, and importance in sixteen-year-old Gene's imagination. He does this in the first line of his flashback to the crucial summer of 1942, the flashback in which practically the entire novel takes place. Gene thinks, "The tree was tremendous, an irate, steely black steeple beside the river. I'd be damned if I'd climb it." Here Knowles has again passed from concrete reality to the heightened language of symbol, and the tree has begun its process of becoming the "focal center of the first part of the novel," and "the Biblical tree of knowledge." Having passed through the writer's creative imagination, a tree which was one of many on a beautiful but quite ordinary New England river bank looms large and lonely, universal and appalling as the tree of the knowledge of good and evil, the tree of both Gene's and Finny's tragic falls.

THE PLAYING FIELDS

As Gene makes his way to the tree, in the opening section of the novel, he passes two buildings, the Gym and the Field House called "The Cage," which are the Thompson Gym and the Thompson Cage of the Academy. Then Knowles has Gene survey "the huge open sweep of ground known as the Playing Fields." Later he says, "Now they reached soggily and emptily away from me, forlorn tennis courts on the left, enormous football and soccer and lacrosse fields in the center, woods on the right, and at the far end a small river detectable from this distance by a few bare trees along its banks." It is a fact that one can see the real courts, fields, woods, and river of the Academy in exactly these positions, but the viewer has to pivot left and put "The Cage" directly in back of him. This minor detail Knowles omits, perhaps because the scene seems vaster when the fields are thought of as beyond, rather than beside, the buildings. Just beyond "The Cage" is a large Service Building, built in 1951. It is easy to understand why Knowles got rid of the latter completely. Even though Gene would have seen it in 1958, it was not there at the time of the conflict and would only be a useless and distracting interpolation.

It is the size of the Playing Fields that seems most to fascinate Gene, and it is only in some exaggeration of their size that Knowles has significantly changed reality. He speaks of Gene's "long trudge across the fields," of "the enormous playing fields," and "the endless green playing fields." And in his first reference to them, Knowles writes, "the playing fields were vast." Gene's trudge from "The Cage" across the baseball and lacrosse fields to the tree is a walk of about 350 yards. This seems to make the fields somewhat less than vast and endless. Also, Gene could have taken a gravel road to the tree and river bank instead of striking out across the fields, if he had walked down to the Service Building and turned left. Again Knowles is clearly heightening. By having Gene walk across muddy fields in the November rain, he makes the scene lonely, threatening, and uncharted. By increasing space, he augments significance, evokes a mood of vastness, and creates a mysterious setting for an action that will turn out to be enormous in consequences and universal in meaning.

Later Knowles will again perform the action of dismissal. He will remove the entire rest of the state of New Hampshire; all the cities and towns and settlements beyond Exeter will not exist in Gene's imagination. The second time the

---

 JOHN KNOWLES ON *A SEPARATE PEACE*

John Knowles comments on how A Separate Peace *grew out of his own life experiences.*

What I set out to do in the novel was to unscramble, plumb, and explain what had happened during a very peculiar summer at Phillips Exeter Academy in New Hampshire, where I was a sixteen-year-old summer-session student in 1943. It was just as World War II was turning in our favor, and were we boys going to be in it or not? And what was war, and what was aggression, and what were loyalty and rivalry, what were goodness and hate and fear and idealism, all of them swirling around us during that peculiar summer?

I wrote the book to dramatize and work through those questions. . . .

I based the narrator, Gene Forrester, on myself; Phineas on my friend, the exceptional student athlete David Hackett. We were in school together for only one summer, at Exeter Academy; his athletic career was conducted at Milton Academy outside Boston and at McGill University in Montreal. There he excelled in many sports, preeminently in hockey, qualifying for the U.S. Olympic Ice Hockey Team in 1948.

Dave was not crippled by a fall from a tree in 1943, but I reversed matters while writing *A Separate Peace* and turned a real, not very serious accident to me into a fateful fictional one for him. This reversal made it possible to show the darker streaks of human nature. If I were going to make my point, then the Phineas character would have to be the victim.

John Knowles, "My Separate Peace," *Esquire*, March 1985.

boys go to the tree, Gene thinks, "Beyond the gym and the fields began the woods, our, the Devon School's woods, which in my imagination were the beginning of the great northern forests. I thought that, from the Devon woods, trees reached in an unbroken, widening corridor so far to the north that no one had ever seen the other end, some where up in the far unorganized tips of Canada. We seemed to be playing on the tame fringe of the last and greatest wilderness." And so they are, symbolically. For on their "tame fringe" and "vast playing fields" they are faced with "the inevitability of evil," and "come to see that this enemy never comes from without, but always from within." By the twin devices of suppression and intensification, Knowles has prepared his setting to bear the weight of so great meaning.

DEVON'S RIVERS

The Phillips Exeter Academy is, like the Devon School, "astride" two rivers. Called the Devon and the Naguamsett in the book, they are the Exeter and the Squamscott on the map of New Hampshire. The Exeter is fresh water, arises inland and joins the salt Squamscott which then flows on to the Great Bay and the Atlantic Ocean. There is a very accurate and quite true description of both in one paragraph of *A Separate Peace.*

> We never used this lower river, the Naguamsett, during the summer. It was ugly, saline, fringed with marsh, mud and seaweed. A few miles away it was joined to the ocean, so that its movements were governed by unimaginable factors like the Gulf Stream, the Polar Ice Cap, and the moon. It was nothing like the fresh-water Devon above the dam where we'd had so much fun, all the summer. The Devon's course was determined by some familiar hills a little inland; it rose among highland farms and forests which we knew, passed at the end of its course through the school grounds, and then threw itself with little spectacle over a small waterfall beside the diving dam, and into the turbid Naguamsett.

Knowles changes the rivers amazingly little in the process of making them symbolic. All he does is constantly emphasize the sweetness and purity, the "dreaming summer calm" of the Exeter-Devon, and the saltiness and ugliness of the Squamscott-Naguamsett. Here he is exaggerating. Today, at least, the Exeter's water is browner and muddier than he makes it; the Squamscott's banks are cleaner. After Gene's quarrel with Cliff Quackenbush during which he falls into the salt river, Gene says, "I had taken a shower to wash off the sticky salt of the Naguamsett River—going into the Devon was like taking a refreshing shower itself, you never had to clean up after it, but the Naguamsett was something else entirely." Again it is by the technique of heightening the real physical characteristics of the two rivers that Knowles, as critics have noted, makes them major symbols of the vast difference between the Summer and Winter Sessions of the Devon School. James Ellis writes:

> What happens in the novel is that Gene Forrester and Phineas, denying the existence of the Second World War as they enjoy the summer peace of Devon School, move gradually into a realization of an uglier adult world—mirrored in the winter and the Naguamsett River—whose central fact is the war. This moving from innocence to adulthood is contained within three sets of interconnected symbols. These three—summer and winter; the Devon River and the Naguamsett River; and peace and war—serve as a backdrop against which the novel is developed, the first of each pair dominating the early novel and giving way to the second only after Gene has discovered the evil of his own heart.

There is an instance of Knowles' technique of omission in his use of the Squamscott River. Since the 1930's there has been a large Academy Boat House on the Squamscott, slightly below the dam at which it is joined by the Exeter. This is the Crew House of the story, the place where Quackenbush holds slightly sinister sway. Knowles does not include in his landscape the large Exeter Manufacturing Company which is on almost the exact opposite bank of the Squamscott and in full view of the Boat House. It is an old and fairly dreary industrial site, which would serve no purpose in Knowles' book. Mentioning it would only introduce the unnecessary life of the surrounding town into this essentially school story. It would not help the mood Knowles was trying to create.

In an article directed toward aspiring writers, which he wrote in 1962, John Knowles tells of the attitude toward writing which he had when he wrote his first novel, *Descent to Proselito*, which was never published. He says that he started by feeling that he had to "mark out the symbolic pattern of my book, and naturally the metaphysical paradoxes." Thornton Wilder later told him that the book was not good because he was "not interested" in it. Knowles continues:

> I now began to write another novel called *A Separate Peace,* and if anything as I wrote tempted me to insert artificial com-

plexities, I ignored it. If anything appeared which looked sus-
piciously like a symbol, I left it on its own. I thought that if I
wrote truly and deeply enough about certain specific people
in a certain place at a particular time having certain specific
experiences, then the result would be relevant for many other
kinds of people and places and times and experiences. I knew
that if I began with symbols, I would end with nothing; if I began with specific individuals, I might end by creating symbols. Yet they were not my concern.

I think that Knowles did write *A Separate Peace* in exactly
this way. He took a specific boys' prep school that he knew
intimately, and, while being amazingly true to almost all its
physical realities, transformed certain of them into symbols
that are never contrived, or artificial, or oppressive. As one
critic has noted, and this inquiry undertakes to demonstrate,
his setting has "both the vitality of verisimilitude and the
psychological tension of symbolism."

Interconnected Symbols

James Ellis

James Ellis identifies three sets of symbols that he
maintains provide the basic structure of *A Separate
Peace*. These paired symbols include summer and
winter, the Devon River and the Naguamsett River,
and peace and war, each of which guides the movement of Gene and Finny from innocence to adulthood and serve as a backdrop against which the
novel can be read and understood. For example,
Gene's baptism in the ugly, marshy Naguamsett
River—in contrast to his experiences in the peaceful
and clean Devon River—occurs after he shakes
Finny from the tree, mirroring his fall from innocence. Ellis was on the faculty of the English department at the University of North Carolina at Greens-
boro when he contributed this essay to the *English
Journal*.

To read *A Separate Peace* is to discover a novel which is completely satisfactory and yet so provocative that the reader
wishes immediately to return to it. John Knowles' achievement is due, I believe, to his having successfully imbued his
characters and setting with a symbolism that while infor-
mative is never oppressive. Because of this the characters
and the setting retain both the vitality of verisimilitude and
the psychological tension of symbolism.

What happens in the novel is that Gene Forrester and
Phineas, denying the existence of the Second World War as
they enjoy the summer peace of Devon School, move gradually to a realization of an uglier adult world—mirrored in
the winter and the Naguamsett River—whose central fact is
the war. This moving from innocence to adulthood is contained within three sets of interconnected symbols. These

Reprinted from James Ellis, "*A Separate Peace:* The Fall from Innocence," *English
Journal*, vol. 53 (1964), pp. 313–18, with permission. Copyright 1964 by the National
Council of Teachers of English.

three—summer and winter; the Devon River and the Naguamsett River; and peace and war—serve as a backdrop against which the novel is developed, the first of each pair dominating the early novel and giving way to the second only after Gene has discovered the evil of his own heart.

The reader is introduced to the novel by a Gene Forrester who has returned to Devon after an absence of fifteen years, his intention being to visit the two sites which have influenced his life—the tree, from which he shook Finny to the earth, and the First Academy Building, in which Finny was made to realize Gene's act. After viewing these two scenes, a "changed" Gene Forrester walks through the rain, aware now that his victory over his internal ignorance is secure. With this realization Gene tells his story of a Devon summer session and its consequences.

THE TREE

Described as ". . . tremendous, an irate, steely black steeple," the tree is a part of the senior class obstacle course in their preparation for war and is the focal center of the first part of the novel. As the Biblical tree of knowledge it is the means by which Gene will renounce the Eden-like summer peace of Devon and, in so doing, both fall from innocence and at the same time prepare himself for the second world war. As in the fall of Genesis, there is concerning this tree a temptation.

Taunted by Phineas to jump from the tree, Gene says: "I was damned if I'd climb it. The hell with it." Aside from its obvious school boy appropriateness, his remark foreshadows his later fall. Standing high in the tree after surrendering to Finny's dare, Gene hears Finny, who had characterized his initial jump as his contribution to the war effort, reintroduce the war motif, saying: "When they torpedo the troopship, you can't stand around admiring the view. Jump!" As Gene hears these words, he wonders: "What was I doing up here anyway? Why did I let Finny talk me into stupid things like this? Was he getting some kind of hold over me?" Then as Gene jumps, he thinks: "With the sensation that I was throwing my life away, I jumped into space."

What Finny represents in Gene's temptation is the pure spirit of man (mirrored in the boy Finny) answering its need to share the experience of life and innocent love. For Finny the war and the tree, which represents a training ground for the war, are only boyish delights. The reality of war is lost upon him because he is constitutionally pure and incapable of malice. That this is so can be seen from Gene's later statement regarding Finny as a potential soldier. He says:

> They'd get you some place at the front and there'd be a lull in the fighting, and the next thing anyone knew you'd be over with the Germans or the Japs, asking if they'd like to field a baseball team against our side. You'd be sitting in one of their command posts, teaching them English. Yes, you'd get confused and borrow one of their uniforms, and you'd lend them one of yours. Sure, that's just what would happen. You'd get things so scrambled up nobody would know who to fight any more. You'd make a mess, a terrible mess, Finny, out of the war.

The tragedy of the novel ultimately is that Gene is not capable of maintaining the spiritual purity that distinguishes Phineas and so must as he discovers his own savagery betray Phineas.

Once the two jumps have been effected, a bond has been cemented between the two. But as Gene and Finny walk up to the dormitories, Gene forgets that he has, in following Finny, denied the adult rules which regulate human relationships, and lapses back into his concern for authority. Falling into his "West Point stride," he says: "We'd better hurry or we'll be late for dinner." Phineas, however, objects to Gene's having forgotten what is exemplified in the jumping from the tree and trips Gene. After a brief scuffle the two boys resume their walk. Gene, then, acknowledges that he has succumbed to Finny. He says:

> Then Finny trapped me again in his strongest trap, that is, I suddenly became his collaborator. As we walked rapidly along, I abruptly resented the bell and my West Point stride and hurrying and conforming. Finny was right.

To acknowledge visibly his giving up the rules of Devon, Gene now trips Finny, and the two are united in a boy's conspiracy to elude adulthood and its rules.

GENE'S ENVY

The progress of the novel after this joining of Phineas and Gene is the progress of Gene's growing envy of Finny. Incapable of the spiritual purity of Phineas, Gene finds himself jealous of Finny's ability to flout Devon rules in his quest to enjoy an "unregulated friendliness" with the adult world. Gene says apropos of several incidents involving Finny and the Devon rules:

I was beginning to see that Phineas could get away with anything. I couldn't help envying him that a little, which was perfectly normal. There was no harm in envying even your best
friend a little.

and

This time he wasn't going to get away with it. I could feel myself becoming unexpectedly excited at that.

And when Finny does evade punishment, Gene thinks:

He had gotten away with everything. I felt a sudden stab of
disappointment. That was because I just wanted to see some
more excitement; that must have been it.

It is during a bicycle trip to the beach on the morning of
the day on which Gene will push Finny from the tree that
Finny confides to Gene that he is his best friend. Gene, however, cannot respond. He says: "I nearly did. But something
held me back. Perhaps I was stopped by that level of feeling,
deeper than thought, which contains the truth." The effect of
this trip is to cause Gene to fail a trigonometry test and
thereby to bring his hatred of Finny into the open. Inventing
reasons to explain what exists only in his projecting it upon
Phineas, Gene says as he realizes what he thinks is Finny's
plot:

Then a second realization broke. . . . Finny had deliberately
set out to wreck my studies. . . . That way he, the great athlete,
would be way ahead of me. It was all cold trickery, it was all
calculated, it was all enmity.

Later, just before he will shake Finny from the tree, Gene
confronts Phineas with his suspicions. Finny's surprise at
the charge is such that Gene realizes its falsity. Confronted
with the evident truth of Finny's denial, Gene understands
his inferiority to Phineas and his own moral ugliness, made
the more so when juxtaposed to Finny's innocence. It is this
realization that prompts his conscious shaking of the tree,
which casts Phineas to the earth and which serves as Gene's
initiation into the ignorance and moral blackness of the human heart.

Returning to the fall session without Phineas, Gene finds
that peace has deserted Devon. And replacing the freedom of
his careless summer are the rules of Devon, to which Gene
now gives his allegiance.

Unable to take part in the boyish activities and sports of
Devon because of his guilt, Gene attempts to find anonymity
in a dead-end job as assistant crew manager. But here, con-

fronted with the arrogance of Cliff Quackenbush (about whom there is an aura of undefined ugliness which separates him from the other boys), Gene is forced to defend Phineas from a slighting remark. This fight between Gene and Quackenbush concludes with their tumbling into the Naguamsett River.

DEVON'S TWO RIVERS

Both the Naguamsett and the Devon flow through the grounds of the school; but it had been into the Devon, a familiar and bucolic river suggestive of Eden, that Finny and Gene had jumped from the tree. But after his fall from innocence, Gene experiences a baptism of a different sort as he plunges into the Naguamsett—a saline, marshy, ugly river "governed by unimaginable factors like the Gulf Stream, the Polar Ice Cap, and the moon."

In what Gene says after his fall into the Naguamsett is introduced the latter parts of the paired symbols that were discussed earlier—the winter, the Naguamsett, and the war (fight). Gene says of his fall:

> I had taken a shower to wash off the sticky salt of the Naguamsett River—going into the Devon was like taking a refreshing shower itself, you never had to clean up after it, but the Naguamsett was something else entirely. I had never been in it before; it seemed appropriate that my baptism there had taken place on the first day of this winter session and that I had been thrown into it, in the middle of a fight.

And just as Gene has gone from the innocence exemplified in the Devon River to the experience of the Naguamsett, so the peaceful Devon River itself, whose course "was determined by some familiar hills a little inland" and which "rose among highland farms and forests," ultimately must succumb to the cosmic force of the world; for it, after passing "at the end of its course through the school grounds," then "threw itself with little spectacle over a small waterfall beside the diving dam and into the turbid Naguamsett."

GENE'S REGENERATION

The return of Phineas to Devon signals the rejuvenation and regeneration of Gene. Immediately prior to Finny's return, Gene had discovered in Brinker's announcement of his intention to enlist a chance to close the door on the pain that has haunted him since his crime against Finny. He says of enlistment and its offer to allow him to consecrate himself to the destruction of the war and to his own capacity for evil:

> To enlist. To slam the door impulsively on the past, to shed everything down to my last bit of clothing, to break the pattern of my life—that complex design I had been weaving alone since birth with all its dark threads, its unexplainable symbols set against a conventional background of domestic white and schoolboy blue, all those tangled strands which required the dexterity of a virtuoso to keep flowing—I yearned to take giant military shears to it, snap! bitten off in an instant, and nothing left in my hands but spools of khaki which could weave only plain, flat, khaki design, however twisted they might be.
>
> Not that it would be a good life. The war would be deadly all right. But I was used to finding something deadly in things that attracted me; there was something deadly lurking in anything I wanted, anything I loved. And if it wasn't there, as for example with Phineas, then I put it there myself.
>
> But in the war, there was no question about it at all; it was there.

But with Phineas' return and Gene's realization that Phineas needs him to help him maintain his integrity, Gene finds moral purpose and determines to live out his life at Devon with Finny. He says:

> Phineas was shocked at the idea of my leaving. In some way he needed me. He needed me. I was the least trustworthy person he had ever met. I knew that; he knew or should know that too. I had even told him. I had told him. But there was no mistaking the shield of remoteness in his face and voice. He wanted me around. The war then passed away from me, and dreams of enlistment and escape and a clean start lost their meaning for me.

With Gene's resolution, peace returns to Devon and the war is forgotten.

A MAKE-BELIEVE WAR

For Phineas, who had even before his fall denied the American bombing of Central Europe, the war is a make-believe—a rumor started by various villains who wish to keep the pure spirit of youth enslaved. Explaining to Gene his vision, Finny points to the roaring twenties "when they all drank bathtub gin and everybody who was young did just what they wanted," and then explains that "the preachers and the old ladies and all the stuffed shirts" stepped in and tried to stop it with Prohibition. But everyone got drunker so they then arranged the depression to keep "the people who were young in the thirties in their places." And when they found "they couldn't use that trick forever," they "cooked up this war fake" for the forties, the *they* now being "the fat old men who don't want us crowding them out of their jobs."

What is important in Finny's theory is that it makes of the war an adult device which curtails the enjoyment of youth and its gifts. To accept the war is for Finny to accept a fallen world. So persuasive is his own illusion and his own magnetic power that Gene is momentarily caught up in it and can deny the war, the denial, however, being occasioned not so much by Finny's explanation as it is by Gene's "own happiness" in having momentarily evaded the ugliness of the war.

The Phineas-inspired Devon Winter Carnival is the occasion during which Gene is to be paraded in all his Olympic glory, signifying that he, through consecrating himself to Finny's tutelage, has become like Phineas. About this winter carnival and his brilliant decathlon performance, Gene says:

> It wasn't the cider which made me surpass myself, it was this liberation we had torn from the gray encroachments of 1943, the escape we had concocted, this afternoon of momentary, illusory, special and separate peace.

Yet even as this illusion is achieved, a telegram arrives from Leper, an "escapee" from the war, come back to destroy Gene's illusion of withdrawing from the war.

At Leper's home in Vermont, Gene finds himself accused of having been responsible for Finny's fall. Later, after the heat of the accusation has passed, the two boys walk in the snow-covered fields while Leper reveals the horror of the military. As he talks, Gene hears the "frigid trees . . . cracking with the cold." To his ears they sound "like rifles being fired in the distance." This paralleling of the trees (the scene of Gene's fall in particular and nature in general) with the war (and hence the ignorance of the human heart, which is responsible for both war and private evil) is given reverberation at Gene's inquisition when Leper describes Gene and Finny as they stood in the tree just before Finny's fall. To Leper they looked "black as death with this fire [the sun] burning all around them; and the rays of the sun were shooting past them, millions of rays shooting past them like—like golden machine-gun fire." Nature then is presented as both damned and damning, with man's death and fall insured by nature's deadly fire and by his own inability to escape the savage within himself.

For Gene, as he listens to Leper, the ugliness of the war finally becomes so forceful that he must run, saying as he does: "I didn't want to hear any more about it. . . . Not now or ever. I didn't care because it had nothing to do with me. And I didn't want to hear any more of it. Ever."

What Gene wants is to return to the world of the winter carnival and his training for the Olympics, his and Phineas' withdrawal from the ugliness of the world. He says:

> I wanted to see Phineas, and Phineas only. With him there was no conflict except between athletes, something Greek-inspired and Olympian in which victory would go to whoever was the strongest in body and heart. This was the only conflict he had ever believed in.

GENE'S UNDERSTANDING

The reconciliation of Gene and Finny after Finny's refusal to accept Brinker's "f——ing facts" and his fall provides the culmination of the novel. Questioned by Finny, Gene denies that his pushing of Phineas was personal. Beginning to understand himself, Gene says: "It was just some ignorance inside me, some crazy thing inside me, something blind, that's all." And joined with this realization is Gene's admission that war, despite Phineas, does exist and that it grows out of the ignorance of the human heart. In rejecting Brinker's thesis that wars can be laid to one's parents and their generation, Gene says: ". . . It seemed clear that wars were not made by generations and their special stupidities, but that wars were made instead by something ignorant in the human heart." Gene has discovered that his private evil, which caused him to hurt Phineas, is the same evil—only magnified—that results in war.

Finny alone, Gene now knows, was incapable of malice. Reviewing his relation with Phineas, Gene tells of Finny's way "of sizing up the world with erratic and entirely personal reservations, letting its rocklike facts sift through and be accepted only a little at a time, only as much as he could assimilate without a sense of chaos and loss."

Because of his ability to admit only as much of the ugliness of life as he could assimilate, Phineas was unique. Gene says:

> No one else I have ever met could do this. All others at some point found something in themselves pitted violently against something in the world around them. With those of my year

this point often came when they grasped the fact of the war. When they began to feel that there was this overwhelmingly hostile thing in the world with them, then the simplicity and unity of their characters broke and they were not the same again.

Phineas alone had escaped this. He possessed an extra vigor, a heightened confidence in himself, a serene capacity for affection which saved him. Nothing as he was growing up at home, nothing at Devon, nothing even about the war had broken his harmonious and natural unity. So at last I had.

It is because of his having known and loved Phineas that Gene can recognize that hatred springs from a greater evil that is within. It is the realization of this that releases him from the hysteria of the war, which now moves from its controlling position off-stage onto the campus of Devon in the form of the parachute riggers.

Unlike his friends who had sought through some building of defenses to ward off the inevitability of evil, Gene has come to see that this enemy never comes from without, but always from within. He knows, moreover, that there is no defense to be built, only an acceptance and purification of oneself through love. Such a love did he share with Phineas in a private gypsy summer. And it is because of the purity of this love that he is able to survive his fall from innocence.

Symbolic Names

Hallman B. Bryant

John Knowles's choice of character names in *A Separate Peace* is highly significant, according to Hallman B. Bryant, an author of many essays on modern American literature. Specifically, the names of the two central characters function on a symbolic level, giving the reader clues to the meaning of their role in the novel. Gene Forrester's name implies that he is well born, athletic, and intelligent. Similarly, a study of biblical history reveals a parallel between the name Phineas and angelic creatures. Not surprisingly, then, Knowles purposefully imbues lofty traits upon the benevolent Phineas.

John Knowles's popular novel, *A Separate Peace*, has a New England boys' school as the unlikely backdrop for a book whose themes are the loss of innocence and original sin. American writers have treated the subject of the fall of man from the very beginning of our literature, and thus Knowles follows a long tradition, but neither this fact nor the larger allegorical structure of the novel is my concern here.

The point I wish to make concerns Knowles's use of descriptive names in *A Separate Peace*, which seems so obvious that I wonder why, so far as I know, no one has yet made it. The two main characters in the novel are two teenaged school boys named Gene and Phineas, and it is the significance of their names that I want to explicate.

GENE: THE GREEK IDEAL

In the case of Gene (whose surname is Forrester), his given name is obviously a shortening of *Eugene*, from the Greek meaning "well-born," implying that the bearer of the name is genetically clean and noble, or at least fortunate in health and antecedents. The idea behind the name ultimately derives from the word *eugenes* from which comes "eugenics,"

Reprinted from Hallman B. Bryant, "Symbolic Names in Knowles's *A Separate Peace*," *Names*, vol. 34 (March 1986), pp. 83–88, with permission. Notes and references in the original have been omitted in this reprint.

the science that deals with the improvement of the hereditary qualities of individuals and races. The implications of Gene's name are apparent in light of his role in the book. He is the narrator as well as the protagonist. His growth and development *vis-a-vis* his relationship with Phineas provide the basic theme. Gene is the ambitious scion of a Southern family whose home is not precisely located but seems to be in Georgia. The Forresters we presume are well off or at least able to afford an expensive eastern prep school for Gene. Thus Gene's surname fits very well with his given name because he does indeed appear to be a well-born Southern aristocrat. Forrester is an English surname that can be traced back to the early Middle Ages, c. 1200's. It derives from the occupation or office of forester, the warden whose duty it was to protect the woods of a lord. The officer was an enforcer, keeper, and custodian. Thus, even Gene's last name suits his role in the novel because he literally becomes a "keeper," first of the dark secret of his guilty act, which crippled Finny; then he keeps up Finny's athletic feats by participating in his stead, and finally he keeps the faith in life that Finny has instilled in him.

It is not only in a social sense that Gene is well born; he is also bright and good at sports, though not so good an athlete as his friend Finny; he appears to embody the Greek ideal of a sound mind in a healthy body, *mens sana in corpore sano*. Gene's appellation also has an ironic aspect because he lacked much while he was growing up despite being well born. From the narrator's account of what he was like when a student at Devon School fifteen years earlier, we learn that he has improved a great deal since the summer of 1942. He has gotten over the fear that haunted him during those years, and he has come through World War II without any scars, either mental, moral, or physical. Gene says, "I began at that point in the emotional examination to note how far my convalescence had gone." As he walks across the campus he notes the way the architecture blends together and wonders, "I could achieve, perhaps unknowingly already had achieved, this growth and harmony myself."

Gene now has "more money and success and 'security' than in days when specters seemed to go with me." He has at last come to terms with himself, yet his rehabilitation was due in no small part to Phineas. Thinking of what he owes his former friend, Gene says, "During the time I was with him, Phineas created an atmosphere in which I continued now to live. . . ."

PHINEAS: SYMBOLIC IMPLICATIONS

Several critics have noted the source and resolution of the tensions that develop between the two boys as well as the numerous Christian symbols in the novel. Much of the ambiguity in their relationship is explained in terms of an allegory of the fall of man. It seems certain that Knowles has an allegorical intention in mind in a plot that features a tree and a series of falls both in the literal, physical and spiritual sense. It seems likewise certain that he chose the names of the two central characters with careful regard for their symbolic meaning as we have already seen in the case of Gene. The choice of the name Phineas even more fully satisfies the meaning of the character's role in the novel. In the first place Phineas is one of those characters in literature and folk culture like Tarzan, Shane, McTeague, and Beowulf who has no last name, which calls attention to the given name and endows it with an added dimension of significance. Secondly, the name *Phineas* is rare in the United States. Even in New England where it was a popular name through the Puritan period, it has steadily died out in the 18th and 19th centuries, and would have been an extremely odd name in the 1940's.

In literary history the name appears in the titles of two of Anthony Trollope's lesser known novels, *The Phineas Finn, the Irish Member* (1869) and *Phineas Redux* (1874). Jules Verne also gave the name to his central character in *Around the World in Eighty Days,* Professor Phineas T. Fogg. There are more remote literary antecedents for the name in Greek mythology, where numerous writers of antiquity, but most prominently Ovid in his *Metamorphosis* mentions a "Phineas" who was a soothsayer-king of Thrace. He was afflicted with blindness by Zeus who was angered because he revealed the future to mortals. Other versions of the myth say Poseidon blinded Phineus for directing Jason and the Argonauts through the Clashing Rocks.

One must go to biblical history, however, to find the kernel of meaning which most applies to the character in Knowles's novel. In the Old Testament there are three figures named Phinehas. The name means "oracle" in Hebrew or "mouth of brass" and is first mentioned in *Exodus* (6:25).

This Phinehas who is the son of Aaron is a judge and priest; a devout keeper of the covenant with the Lord, he gave rise to a line of priests known as "the sons of Phinehas." There is another person named Phinehas, but he is not so exemplary. He is the youngest son of Eli, a rebellious youth who was a rule breaker; he redeemed himself by protecting the Ark. The third individual who bears the name Phinehas is an angel, and it is this figure who has the most bearing upon the Phineas in the novel. In the book of Judges (2:1) the youngest of the 72 angels of the Lord "who comes up from Gilad" is called Phinehas. This angel's "countenance glowed like a torch when the light of the Holy Ghost rested upon it," the Scripture says. It is interesting to note at this juncture that an angel is by definition a presence whose powers transcend the logic of our existence. Also as St. Augustine wrote, "Every visible thing in this world is put under the charge of an angel."

While it might be possible to make a tangential application of the careers of the first two biblical characters to the situation of Phineas in the novel, it is the shared nature of the angel Phinehas in the Bible and the boy Phineas in Knowles's book that I wish to examine.

PHINEAS AS GUARDIAN ANGEL

I do not think that it is stretching a point to say that Gene has come to believe that Phineas was his guardian angel. After Phineas has died Gene says "he [Phineas] was present in every moment of every day...." He at this point is convinced that his friend "Finny" has given him a standard of conduct and credo that will save him from the negative emotions created by a world at war. At the end of the novel as the Army Parachute Riggers school marches in to set up operations at Devon, Gene falls into step with their cadence count; however, he is really marching to the beat of a different drummer: "My feet of course could not help but begin to fall involuntarily into step with the coarse voice [of the drill sergeant]," but "down here [in his soul] I fell into step as well as my nature, Phineas filled, would allow." Although Gene will walk to the cadence that the world calls, he will also keep step to the credo of the good and guileless Finny, who like an angel was really too good to live in this world. As Gene declared earlier, speaking to Finny in the infirmary shortly after his fall down the marble steps, "You wouldn't be any good in the war, even if nothing had happened to your leg." What Gene means here is that Finny's spirit was naturally benevolent rather than bellicose; he adds, "They'd get you some place at the front and there'd be a lull in the fighting, and the next thing anyone knew you'd be over with the Germans or the Japs, asking them if they'd like to field a baseball team against our side. . . . You'd get things so scrambled up nobody would know who to fight any more."

Finny shares numerous other angelic traits with his namesake. The angel Phinehas was remarkable for his compelling voice and his face with glowing features. Phineas is described in the early chapters in remarkably similar terms. Gene says of his voice, "It was the equivalent in sound of a hypnotist's eyes." And again, speaking of Finny—"He rambled on, his voice soaring and plunging in its vibrant sound box. . . ." Describing Finny participating in class discussions, Gene says, "When he was forced to speak himself the hypnotic power of his voice combined with the singularity of his mind to produce answers which were not often right but could rarely be branded as wrong." In addition to a remarkable voice, Finny's glowing green eyes light up his face. When excited his green eyes widen and he has a maniac look; we are told that his "eyes flash green across the room and that he blazed with sunburned health." In the longest description given of Finny's face Gene notes his friend's odd appearance: "Phineas had soaked and brushed his hair for the occasion. This gave his head a sleek look, which was contradicted by the surprised, honest expression which he wore on his face. His ears, I had never noticed before, were fairly small and set close to his head, and combined with his plastered hair they now gave his bold nose and cheekbones the sharp look of a prow."

When one reviews the peculiar physiognomy of Phineas as well as the suggestions raised by his hypnotic voice, vivid blue-green eyes, and his extrasensory hearing, it seems that the evidence of an angelic parallel is inescapable. Angels traditionally are endowed with supernatural and seeming magic powers of voice and eye which they use to enthrall their listeners; also, angels according to medieval lore have fine ears in order to hear the music of the spheres. Furthermore, the sleek, shiplike features of Phineas are in keeping with early Christian angel iconography as is his skin, "which radiates a reddish copper glow." Finally, there is one more facet of analogy that pertains here. Angels, according to the doctrines of the early church, were immortal but not eternal. Also it was held that virtuous men could attain angelic rank. While no mention is made of Finny in the next world in *A Separate Peace,* it is apparent that he was an influence, if not necessarily a supernatural one, a nonetheless benevolent one who in the role of Gene's savior plays the part of an angel in deed as well as in name.

"A GRACE BEYOND THE REACH OF ART"

Whether Knowles intended for Phineas to be linked with precursors who bore this name in scripture, myth, and Christian legends of angels, it is not possible to say. However, it is a matter of record that Knowles writes to challenge the reader. In an essay entitled "The Young Writer's Real Friends," he says, "I think readers should work more. I don't want to imagine everything for them." In the same essay he tries to answer critics who charged him with writing over-intellectualized novels and he refers directly to how he wrote *A Separate Peace*:

> . . . if anything as I wrote tempted me to insert intellectual complexities I ignored it. If anything appeared which looked suspiciously like a symbol, I left it on its own. I thought that if I wrote truly and deeply enough about certain people in a certain place at a particular time having a certain experience, then the result would be relevant to many other kinds of people and places and times and experiences. . . . I know that if I began with symbols, I would end with nothing; if I began with certain individuals I might end up by creating symbols.

Thus it is that the names of both Gene and "Finny" are aptly chosen; whether by design or "a grace beyond the reach of art," they seem perfectly natural and inconspicuous names on the literal level and yet also function symbolically, focusing the theme of the novel even more clearly, if what is in the name is understood.

CHAPTER 2

Technique in *A Separate Peace*

Narrative Method

Ronald Weber

"Looking back now across fifteen years, I could see with great clarity the fear I had lived in," says the narrator Gene early in *A Separate Peace*. Critic Ronald Weber notes that this time lapse is significant. By looking back over fifteen years, the mature Gene is able to accurately interpret events for the reader of *A Separate Peace*. Moreover, even when the narrative reverts to immediate scene, Knowles deliberately reminds the reader of the time lapse. This narrative method, according to Weber, makes the novel's theme—that one can find peace from fear only through understanding and acceptance—both possible and plausible. Weber was an assistant professor in the department of Communications at the University of Notre Dame when he contributed this article to *Studies in Short Fiction*.

[In *A Separate Peace*]Gene Forrester is separated by a broad passage of time from the experience he relates. "I went back to the Devon School not long ago," Gene says in the novel's opening sentence, "and found it looking oddly newer than when I was a student there fifteen years before." That this lapse in time between the experience and the telling has brought understanding is also established early. "Looking back now across fifteen years," Gene says a few paragraphs later, "I could see with great clarity the fear I had lived in. . . ." Although Knowles quickly leaves the distant perspective and turns to immediate scene, he keeps the reader aware that Gene is looking back on the experience with a mature vision. At one point, for example, the distant perspective suddenly opens up at the end of a scene when Gene says: "But in a week I had forgotten that, and I have never since forgotten the dazed look in Finny's face when he thought that on the first day of his return to Devon I was go-

Excerpted from Ronald Weber, "Narrative Method in *A Separate Peace*," *Studies in Short Fiction*, vol. 3, no. 1 (Fall 1965), pp. 63–72. Copyright 1965 by Newberry College. Reprinted with permission. Notes and references in the original have been omitted in this reprint.

ing to desert him." Later, beginning a chapter, Knowles reëstablishes the perspective with a long passage that again looks ahead of the present action:

> That night I made for the first time the kind of journey which later became the monotonous routine of my life: traveling through an unknown countryside from one unknown settlement to another. The next year this became the dominant activity, or rather passivity, of my army career, not fighting, not marching, but this kind of nighttime ricochet; for as it turned out I never got to the war.

THE BENEFIT OF EXPERIENCE

The distant point of the narration allows a detachment that permits Gene the mastery of his experience. Even when Knowles gives over the narrative wholly to immediate scene the reader is reminded, sometimes with a phrase, at other times with an entire passage, of the perspective. The war, in addition, serves to create an increased sense of distance, a removal in attitude, within the story. Although the war touches Devon School only slightly—one of the joys of the summer session is that it seems totally removed from the world of war—it cannot be forgotten or ignored for long; it exists not only as an event that stands between the experience of the novel and Gene's telling, but as an event that, at the very moment of the experience, dominates the life of each character. "The war," Gene says in retrospect, "was and is reality for me. I still instinctively live and think in its atmosphere." The anticipation of war forces Gene and his companions into a slight yet significant detachment from their life at Devon—a life that, at times, seems unimportant and even unreal—and towards an unusual amount of serious, if carefully guarded, reflection. The relation between the fact of war and the atmosphere of detachment or removal in the novel—removal, again, necessary for understanding—can be seen in Phineas' disclosure that, despite his humorous disavowal of the existence of the war, he has been trying for some time to enlist:

> I'll *hate* it *everywhere* if I'm not in this war [he tells Gene]! Why do you think I kept saying there wasn't any war all winter? I was going to keep on saying it until two seconds after I got a letter from Ottawa or Chungking or some place saying, "Yes, you can enlist with us. . . ." Then there would have been a war.

Similarly, the war serves to remove Gene from his immediate experience and to provoke serious self-scrutiny:

To enlist [he thinks in response to a day spent freeing snow-bound trains in a railroad yard as part of the war effort]. To slam the door impulsively on the past, to shed everything down to my last bit of clothing, to break the pattern of my life—that complex design I had been weaving since birth with all its dark threads, its unexplainable symbols set against a conventional background of domestic white and schoolboy blue, all those tangled strands which required the dexterity of a virtuoso to keep flowing—I yearned to take giant military shears to it, snap! bitten off in an instant, and nothing left in my hands but spools of khaki which could weave only a plain, flat, khaki design, however twisted they might be.

The depth of insight revealed in the passage is made possible both by the narrator's removal in time from the experience and by the existence within the experience of the war as a focus of attention outside of him. Finally, the passage suggests how the central dramatic event of the story, Gene's involvement in the injury of Phineas, adds to the atmosphere of detachment in the novel. The injury, which occurs early in the story and underlies the bulk of the narrative, is another force thrusting Gene away from his immediate experience and towards self-scrutiny; as such, it combines with the distant point of the narration and the existence of war to create the broad quality of detachment that makes understanding both possible and plausible.

Gene comes to self-understanding only gradually through a series of dramatic episodes, as we shall see; the final extent of his understanding can, however, be indicated by a passage from the concluding chapter. "I was ready for the war," he says, thinking ahead to his entry into the army, "now that I no longer had any hatred to contribute to it. My fury was gone, I felt it gone, dried up at the course, withered and lifeless.". . .

FEAR AND ESCAPE

At this point we can begin to see some connection between Knowles's narrative method and his thematic concern. . . .

At the very beginning of the novel, in a passage quoted earlier, Gene, looking back fifteen years, says he can see with great clarity the "fear" he had lived in at Devon School and that he has succeeded in making his "escape" from. Even now, he adds, he can feel "fear's echo," and this in turn leads him back to the direct experience of the story. The meaning of this experience is to be found in the development of the words *fear* and *escape*—in Gene's growing realization of what they mean as well as what they do not mean.

When his friend and roommate Phineas breaks a Devon swimming record and then refuses to let anyone know about it, Gene is deeply troubled:

> Was he trying to impress me or something? Not tell anybody? When he had broken a school record without a day of practice? I knew he was serious about it, so I didn't tell anybody. Perhaps for that reason his accomplishment took root in my mind and grew rapidly in the darkness where I was forced to hide it.

Later, during an overnight escapade on an oceanside beach, Phineas causes him another moment of uncertainty. Just before the two boys fall asleep, Phineas frankly declares that Gene is his "best pal."

> It was a courageous thing to say [Gene reflects]. Exposing a sincere emotion nakedly like that at the Devon School was the next thing to suicide. I should have told him then that he was my best friend also and rounded off what he had said. I started to; I nearly did. But something held me back. Perhaps I was stopped by that level of feeling, deeper than thought, which contains the truth.

Gene's troubled feelings rise to the level of thought in a following scene during which he comes to the conclusion that Phineas, the school's finest athlete, envies him his academic success. This knowledge instantly shatters any notions he has had of "affection and partnership and sticking by someone and relying on someone absolutely in the jungle of a boys' school." He now sees that Phineas is his rival, not his friend, and this in turn explains his failure to respond properly when Phineas broke the swimming record and when he confessed his friendship. He now sees that he has been envious of Phineas too—envious to the point of complete enmity. Out of the wreck of their friendship this dual rivalry emerges as a saving bit of knowledge:

> I found it [Gene says]. I found a single sustaining thought. The thought was, You and Phineas are even already. You are even in enmity. You are both coldly driving ahead for yourselves alone. You did hate him for breaking that school swimming record, but so what? He hated you for getting an A in every course but one last term.

Their mutual hatred not only explains Gene's inability to respond properly to Phineas, but it relieves him of any further anxiety:

A SEQUEL TO *A SEPARATE PEACE*
Hallman B. Bryant comments on Peace Breaks Out, *John Knowles's sequel to* A Separate Peace.

Readers of *A Separate Peace* might be interested to know that Knowles wrote a sequel to his first novel entitled *Peace Breaks Out*, published by Holt, Rhinehart and Winston in 1981. While the new book depends on *A Separate Peace*, none of the characters from the first book appear. It does retain the Devon school as a setting and again uses the prep school as a microcosm to focus on the larger issues of human existence. As *A Separate Peace* concerns itself with a group of schoolboys trying to deal with the pressures of a world at war, *Peace Breaks Out* shows students at Devon trying to find a basis for life in a world after war. Knowles's point in the sequel is that peace can bring mixed blessings. The nation, having defeated all external enemies, now moves to eliminate all internal foes, real or imagined. Here the enemy is depicted as those who would corrupt the "Devon Spirit," which is obviously intended to parallel the paranoia that beset the country in the McCarthy era, when witchhunting government committees were seeking out cases of anti-Americanism.

Hallman B. Bryant, *A Separate Peace: The War Within*, Boston: Twayne, 1990.

I felt better. Yes, I sensed it like the sweat of relief when nausea passes away; I felt better. We were even after all, even in enmity. The deadly rivalry was on both sides after all.

Gene's sense of relief, it turns out, is of short duration. When Phineas, in a moment of seriousness, urges him to stick with his studies rather than come along on a campus diversion, Gene suddenly sees he has been wrong—Phineas has never envied him. During a scene immediately following, in which he and Phineas perch in a tree waiting to leap into a river below, Gene is overwhelmed by the implications of this new insight:

Any fear I had ever had of the tree was nothing beside this. It wasn't my neck, but my understanding which was menaced. He had never been jealous of me for a second. Now I knew that there never was and never could have been any rivalry between us. I was not of the same quality as he. I couldn't stand this.

It is at this moment that he causes Phineas to fall from the tree, an "accident" that cripples him and ends his athletic career. After watching Phineas crash through the branches of the tree and hit the bank Gene jumps confidently into the river, "every trace of my fear of this forgotten."

THE DISCOVERY OF HATE

It is Phineas' innocence that Gene cannot endure. As long as he can believe Phineas shares his enmity, he can find relief; but with this assurance gone, he stands condemned before himself and must strike out against his tormentor. *Fear*, again, is the key word. Fear in this instance is the emotional response to the discovery of hate, the vast depths of enmity that exist within the human heart. Gene loses his fear and achieves his separate, personal peace only when he acknowledges this fundamental truth. It is a truth that he must first recognize and then accept; he can neither avoid it, as he tries to do in his first encounter with Phineas after the accident, nor flee from it, as he again seeks to do when Leper charges that he always has been a "savage underneath." He can find escape from fear only in the acceptance of its true source and the location of that source. Gene must come to see and endure the truth, as he finally does in a climactic scene just before Phineas dies from a second fall, that his fear is the product not of rivalry nor of circumstance but of "some ignorance inside me, some crazy thing inside me, something blind."

None of Gene's companions at Devon could bring themselves to face this inner source of their fear. When they began to feel this "overwhelmingly hostile thing in the world with them," they looked beyond themselves and felt themselves violently pitted against something in the outer world. When they experienced this "fearful shock" of the "sighting of the enemy," they began an "obsessive labor of defense" and began to parry the menace they thought they saw facing them. They all

> constructed at infinite cost to themselves these Maginot Lines against this enemy they thought they saw across the frontier, this enemy who never attacked that way—if he ever attacked at all; if he was indeed the enemy.

The infinite cost in this case is the loss of self-knowledge. Only Phineas is an exception; only Phineas "never was afraid" because only he "never hated anyone." Phineas alone is free of the awareness of that hostile thing that is to be found not across any battlefield but within the fortress itself. As the archetypal innocent, he must serve as the sacrifice to

Gene's maturity. "I was ready for the war," Gene says at the end, "now that I no longer had any hatred to contribute to it. My fury was gone. . . . Phineas had absorbed it and taken it with him, and I was rid of it forever."

Gene Forrester comes to learn that his war, the essential war, is fought out on the battlefield within. Peace comes only when he faces up to this fact. The only escape, the price of peace, is self-awareness.

Counterpoint

James M. Mellard

Critic James M. Mellard finds a pattern of counter-poised elements in *A Separate Peace*. For example, the idyllic peace of Devon is set against the harsh reality of World War II. As war overtakes peace, seasonal symbolism, too, becomes dualistic; Knowles contrasts the dreamlike gypsy summer with the harsh, frozen dead of winter. The relationship between Finny and Gene—two antithetical characters searching for personal fulfillment—also displays this symbolic counterpoint. By using counterpoint in character development, symbolism, plot and structure, Knowles supports and heightens the novel's basic theme: the loss of innocence and growth to maturity. Mellard was on the faculty of the English Department at the University of Southern California. He has published several articles in literary journals.

A Separate Peace, John Knowles's first novel and winner of the first William Faulkner Foundation Award, has become one of the most popular books for literary study in American education since its publication in 1960. The novel is narrated from the point of view of a man looking back over fifteen years at the climactic events of his youth at a New England preparatory school. This retrospective point of view enables Knowles, like [F. Scott] Fitzgerald in *The Great Gatsby*, to present a dual perspective of characters, events, symbols, and settings. Akin, in fact, to the movement of Knowles's recent non-fictional *Double Vision* (1965), the direction of the narrative in the novel is toward the protagonist's recognition and acceptance of a puzzling duality, a "double vision," at the very heart of existence. And because of theme and point of view, the demands of symbolism, characterization, and narrative in *A Separate Peace* make counterpoint the most important technique in Knowles's fiction.

From James M. Mellard, "Counterpoint and 'Double Vision' in *A Separate Peace*," *Studies in Short Fiction*, vol. 4, no. 2 (Winter 1967), pp. 127–34. Copyright 1967 by Newberry College. Reprinted with permission. Notes and references in the original have been omitted in this reprint.

Arising naturally from setting, the novel's contrapuntal symbolism operates organically in the development of its theme, the growth to maturity through the loss of adolescent innocence and the acceptance of adult experience. The basic symbolism is the contrast between the peace of the school and the war going on outside, for it provides the objective correlative for the subjective battles fought by the youthful characters as they search for personal fulfillment. It is against the war, therefore, that Gene Forrester, the central and point-of-view character of the novel, directs most of his thoughts. To Gene, "The war was and is reality"; and for much of the novel, it is the hard world of reality, of the war, that Gene, at times only unconsciously, hopes to evade, a desire he manages to fulfill during most of the final school year, through the intervention of his friend Phineas, or "Finny," as he is usually called. Gene says, for example, that "the war swept over like a wave at the seashore, gathering power and size as it bore on us, overwhelming in its rush, seemingly inescapable, and then at the last moment eluded by a word from Phineas . . . ." Yet the war, like growth and maturity, can hardly be avoided forever, because "one wave is inevitably followed by another even larger and more powerful, when the tide is coming in." So the youths at Devon, and particularly Gene, enjoy their "momentary, illusory, special and separate peace" whenever they can, just as, during Devon's first Summer Session, the faculty relaxed its controls on the boys because they "reminded them of what peace was like."

SEASONAL COUNTERPOINT

The fundamental counterpoint between war and peace, reality and illusion, is made more immediate in the symbolic contrast between the "gypsy" summer and the "unromantic" winter. Members of the only summer session in Devon's history, Gene, Phineas and the others make the best of it, managing to break most of the school's rules while still maintaining the faculty's good will playing at warfare, making up chaotic new games, such as "Blitzball," and forming new clubs, like the "Super Suicide Society of the Summer Session." Supporting the contrast between the reality of the war and the illusions of peace, the opposition between summer and winter is essentially a balancing of the world of fantasy, dream, and desire against the world of fact, even of night-

mare and repulsion. As long as the summer lasts, the sense
of peace and fulfillment and happiness conquers the en-
croachments of the war, with its defeats, frustrations and
pain: "Bombs in Central Europe were completely unreal to
us here, not because we couldn't imagine it . . . but because
our place here was too fair for us to accept something like
that . . . ." But just as another wave will follow the one
eluded, the Winter Session will replace the Summer Session:
"It had been the school's first, but this was its one hundred
and sixty-third Winter Session, and the forces assembled for
it scattered the easygoing summer spirit like so many fallen
leaves." At the first Chapel of the new session, Gene thinks
how Devon had changed during the summer, how "tradi-
tions had been broken, the standards let down, all rules forgotten," but he also realizes that the summer is past, that ret-
ribution awaits:

> Ours had been a wayward gypsy music, leading us down all
> kinds of foolish gypsy ways, unforgiven. I was glad of it, I had
> almost caught the rhythm of it, the dancing, clicking jangle of
> it during the summer.

> Still it had come to an end, in the last long rays of daylight at
> the tree, when Phineas fell. It was forced upon me as I sat
> chilled through the Chapel service, that this probably vindi-
> cated the rules of Devon after all, wintery Devon. If you broke
> the rules, then they broke you. That, I think, was the real
> point of the sermon on this first morning.

And at this juncture, with school beginning, the summer
over, Phineas gone and unlikely to return because of a shattered leg, and the too, too real world of the war reasserting
itself, Gene gives himself to the disturbing thought that the
"idiosyncratic, leaderless band" of the summer would soon
be back under the control of the "official class leaders and
politicians." But because the "gypsy days" had intervened
and he had absorbed much from Finny, Gene attempts to
fight the world alone, a personal battle doomed to failure,
but which has momentary triumphs after Finny returns to
guide him. The climax of this battle, the "Winter Carnival,"
is itself a result of the contrast between winter and summer
and Gene's desire to restore the spirit of the past summer in
the dead of winter. "On this Saturday at Devon," Gene says,
"there was going to be no government," and "on this day
even the schoolboy egotism of Devon was conjured away."
At the Winter Carnival, just before the news of Leper's army

desertion, Gene comes closest to regaining the summer place beside his friend Phineas. But this idyllic interlude is followed immediately by Gene's journey through the demonic wintry wasteland of northern New England to see Leper, a trip which reasserts the fact of the war.

DEVON'S TWO RIVERS

Another use of counterpoint and one even more specific than the seasonal symbolism is the antithesis between the two rivers that run through the Devon campus and that make the school itself part of the dualistic symbolism. As the summer connotes peace and dream and fantasy, the Devon River represents goodness, beauty, even purity: "going into the Devon was like taking a refreshing shower itself, you never had to clean up after it." It is associated with the cultivated, the pastoral, the idyllic, with the "familiar hills," the "highland farms and forests we knew." The "turbid" Naguamsett, associated with winter, suggests everything contrary to the spirit of the Devon: it is "ugly, saline, fringed with marsh," and it is "governed by unimaginable factors." But as the war overtakes peace, and winter replaces summer, the highland Devon must drop into the lowland Naguamsett, a vicissitude which suggests once again that youth cannot avoid the responsibilities of maturity. So, if the events of the "gypsy summer" take place beside and in the Devon, the events of the winter must take place beside and in the Naguamsett. And where the central image of the summer is Gene and his "best pal" Phineas leaping together into the Devon, in a gesture of brotherhood, the key image of the winter session is Gene and Quackenbush catapulting into the Naguamsett, "in the middle of a fight."

A CONTRAPUNTAL RELATIONSHIP

In addition to the symbolic counterpoint arising from the temporal and physical settings, contrapuntal character relationships control the development of theme and structure. The major character conflict is that which Gene imagines to exist between him and Finny. Like the novel's symbolism, this conflict grows rather naturally from the setting, for a sense of rivalry often prevails in such schools as Devon. Superficially, it is based upon the school's dual emphasis on athletics and scholarship, because Finny is by far the school's best athlete, while Gene is close to being its very

best student. Once Gene decides that they are rivals and that
Finny has been artfully concealing his ambitions and attempting to wreck his studies, he decides that they are enemies as well, and, like it or not, they "are even in enmity."
But the conflict between Finny and Gene goes much deeper
than this, for there are essential oppositions in personality.
The fundamental contrast is simply that Gene is all too human and heir to all the weaknesses of flesh and spirit, while
Finny, at least as Gene sees him most of the time, is little less
than a divinity. Thus where Gene is at times morally and
ethically shallow, Finny is the epitome of honesty and open-
ness and fidelity. And yet, of the two, Finny is the noncon-
formist, for his values are generally self-created, although
they never seem self-interested. Thus Gene says,

> . . . I noticed something about Finny's own mind, which was
> such an opposite from mine. It wasn't completely unleashed
> after all. I noticed that he did abide by certain rules, which he
> seemed to cast in the form of commandments. "Never say you
> are five feet nine when you are five feet eight and a half" was
> the first one I encountered. Another was, "Always say some
> prayers at night because it might turn out there is a God."

This last "Commandment" is a good illustration of the quality
of Finny's mind, for it in no way represents a self-protective
covering of his bets; on the contrary, it shows Finny's desire to
see the world as it ought to be; hence Gene's memories are of
"Phineas losing even in those games he invented, betting always for what *should* win, for what would have been the most
brilliant successes of all, if only the cards hadn't betrayed him."
Gene, on the other hand, usually played conservatively, aware
at all times of percentages, rules, conventions; consequently, to
Gene one of the most astounding of Finny's feats is not so
much his breaking a school swimming record without a day
of practice, but his unwillingness to have it publicized or even
officially recognized, for what Gene values most, at least in the
beginning, is conventional and public approval. Thus while
Finny has relative values, Gene's values are absolute; where
"Finny's life was ruled by inspiration and anarchy," Gene's
"was subject to the dictates of [his] own mind, which gave
[him] the maneuverability of a strait jacket." And where Finny
is the "essence of . . . peace," freedom, courage and selflessness, Gene, until he becomes, as it were, a part of Finny, is
swayed by some "ignorance" inside him and trapped by his
own guilt and fear and egotism.

Although Knowles insists upon the contrasts between Finny and Gene, he also shows that the two antithetical personalities can, even must, merge into one, just as summer slides into winter, the Devon into the Naguamsett, peace into war. But if these changes seem to be governed by something absolute and unfathomable and yet seem to create something better out of a process that appears undesirable, Gene's transformation also seems to result in a being of greater durability, if not of goodness, one better able to keep his balance in a chaotic world than either the original Gene or Finny. To Gene, Finny is a god, a god of the river, as his name suggests. But, god or man, Finny is not, as Gene tells him, suited for the world as it is, for the war and, thus, for reality. Hence, Phineas, besides his initial contrast to Gene, even points to a strong contrapuntal character symbolism: both the representative of Gene's "fall from innocence" and grace and the means for his deliverance and redemption, in a novel filled with Christian symbols and a theme linked to the concepts of original sin and the fortunate fall, Phineas becomes both Adam and Christ, the "second Adam," in a concentrated, powerful symbolism that is paradoxical, but also traditionally Christian. And, "Phineas-filled" at the novel's conclusion, Gene is enabled to size up the world, like Phineas, "with erratic and entirely personal reservations, letting its rocklike facts sift through and be accepted only a little at a time, only as much as he could assimilate without a sense of chaos and loss."

FINNY'S TWO FALLS

The uses of counterpoint in symbolism and characterization are important, but they by no means complete *A Separate Peace*. Of equal significance are the contrapuntal devices of plot and structure. There are many actions that have their counteractions in the novel, but the major counterpointed scenes are those that involve Finny's two falls, the markers that determine the three-part structure of the novel. As in symbolism and characterization, the structure of the novel shows a kind of dialectical movement, first revealing the antitheses between the two central figures, then suggesting the "transformation" of one, Gene, into his opposite, and finally portraying, in dramatically convincing ways, the reconciliation of the opposites into one unified, complete and well adjusted personality, who, better than most, can come to terms with the dual attractions of the world.

The climax of part one, at the end of Chapter Four, is the fall of Phineas from the tree beside the Devon River, but it is prepared for by Gene's increasing suspicions and sense of rivalry. Gene's erroneous but nevertheless powerful distrust of Finny begins to emerge when he watches a sunrise at the beach, after Finny had inveigled him to skip school; it culminates when Gene, in a realization that "broke as clearly and bleakly as dawn at the beach," decides that his friend "had deliberately set out to wreck" his studies so that they would not be even. Shortly after, however, at the tree where the "Suicide Society" members test their devotion to the club, Gene recognizes his tremendous spiritual isolation and physical fear, for, although he cannot yet understand why, he realizes that Finny "had never been jealous . . . for a second." So now he realizes more than ever that he "was not of the same quality" as Phineas, a "truth," however, that he cannot abide at all. Moments later, Gene shakes the limb on which they are balancing and causes Finny to fall. The counterpart to this scene of "crime," at the center of which is a ritual test of personal and idiosyncratic values, is the scene of "punishment," the trial that precedes the second fall at the end of Chapter Eleven. The trial reverses the implications of the first fall, for it indicates Gene's progress away from isolation toward social integration.

Just as the scenes preceding the falls are contrasted, the results of the falls are also carefully counterpointed. The major contrast is in the reversal of the influences upon Gene and Phineas: the first fall is far more important to Gene than to Finny, for while it causes physical anguish for Finny, it creates a much greater emotional anguish for Gene. His anguish releases him from fear, but it creates a social guilt and alienation and a corresponding need to identify completely with Phineas, to "become" Phineas, as it were, in order to escape himself. But as Gene grows more and more sure of himself, of his own identity and "real authority and worth," he comes to depend less and less upon Phineas, who was, because of his disability, so dependent upon Gene that he thought of Gene as an "extension of himself." Consequently, the second fall has far greater ramifications for Finny than for Gene. After this accident, Finny is forced to acknowledge the existence of "something blind" in man's character and to accept the fact that Gene caused his original fall because of "some kind of blind impulse." If the ultimate effect of the two falls upon Gene was to make him more capable of existing in the "real" world, their contrary effect upon Finny was simply to destroy him: as Gene had told him long before, Phineas was "too good to be true," so there really could be no place in the world for him, no matter how hard he or Gene might wish it.

GENE'S TRANSFORMATION

Although Phineas is its most memorable character, *A Separate Peace* is Gene's story, and the point of that story is Gene's growing into maturity and accepting his place in the world. Consequently, the most important scene for Gene, after the falls, is his inevitable but painful recognition of the world's and his own duality. This recognition involves the contrast of his youthful, adolescent, "old" way of viewing the world with a more mature, adult, "new" way. Occurring just after Phineas' accident on the stairs, in the building where "boys come to be made men," this scene is the literal and symbolic aftermath of Finny's rejection of Gene. It is actually the climax of the novel because Gene's emotional rejection of Finny's way of life is more important than Finny's death; it shows Gene taking a midnight walk through the campus and sleeping overnight in the stadium. During his walk, Gene says, "I was trying to cope with something that might be called double vision. I saw the gym in the glow of a couple of outside lights near it and I knew of course that it was the Devon gym which I entered every day. It was and it wasn't. There was something innately strange about it, as though there had always been an inner core to the gym which I had never perceived before, quite different from its generally accepted appearance." This "double vision" is true of all else that he sees; everything has a "significance much deeper and far more real than any" he had noticed before, taking on meanings, "levels of reality," he had never suspected. His first impression is that he himself lacked reality, that he was a "ghost," a "dream," a "figment which had never really touched anything." But his real problem as well as his most pressing need are revealed when he says, "I felt that I was not, never had been and never would be a living part of this overpoweringly solid and deeply meaningful world around me."

After the night's sleep in the stadium and the awakening to a fresh new perspective on existence, however, Gene walks back to the "center of the school," has breakfast, gets a notebook from his room and goes to class, actions that suggest powerfully that he has given up Phineas and the stadium, as it were, for his own identity and the classroom. Only now is he enabled again to face Finny with the truth about his first catastrophe and, shortly afterward, to accept, almost without pain, the fact of Finny's death. And it is only after his becoming aware of a double view of reality that Gene steps over the threshold of maturity, now able to recognize existence for what it is, to accept his own position in the world; and to go to war without fear or hatred.

If Phineas has "absorbed" the worst of Gene and taken it with him, Gene has himself absorbed and taken with him the best of Finny—"a way of sizing up the world." Although Gene can "never agree with either" Brinker's or Finny's view of the world ("It would have been comfortable, but I could not believe it."), at least Finny's way of sizing it up with "erratic and entirely personal reservations" allowed one to maintain a coherent, integrated personality. But the key word here is *personal*—one must remain true to himself, his own identity, fulfill his own possibilities rather than another's. So if Gene can never be as innocent as Phineas or regain their "paradise lost," he can at least measure others, as well as himself, against Phineas as he measured the world against Devon, in that prelapsarian summer of 1942. And if he and the others fall short of Finny's standard, as they must, they will still gain from having reached for it.

Dual Perspective Narrative

Ian Kennedy

John Knowles narrates *A Separate Peace* through two
distinct time periods of the same person's life: Gene
the boy and Gene the man. In the following essay, Ian
Kennedy writes that this method overcomes the limitations of first-person narration and provides the
reader with a highly effective dual perspective. The
young Gene conveys freshness and vitality in his narration of events, yet he is too immature to accurately
interpret his experiences. In contrast, the older Gene
is too removed from events—fifteen years have
elapsed—to describe them with the sense of immediacy imparted by his younger counterpart. Yet it is the
older Gene who corrects the younger Gene's unreliable commentary and provides the basis for the
reader's understanding of *A Separate Peace*. Kennedy
has taught at Southwest Missouri State University.

A Separate Peace is narrated by two Gene Forresters, one of
whom conveys the actions, feelings, and thoughts of the moment, while the other looks back on that turmoil from a distance
of fifteen years and provides intelligent and illuminating comments. Gene the boy is too close to his own experiences to understand them properly, and Gene the man is too removed to express effectively the vitality that characterizes adolescence, but
between them they succeed in dissolving the limitations of conventional first-person narration. Although it is true that this
method is not conventional, Knowles is not, however, breaking
new ground; for after numerous explorations and experiments
in first-person narrative, [Charles] Dickens adopted this method
of dual perspective in his telling of *Great Expectations*, in which
there can be found much the same balanced oscillation be-

Abridged from Ian Kennedy, "Dual Perspective Narrative and the Character of Phineas
in *A Separate Peace*," *Studies in Short Fiction*, vol. 11, no. 1 (Fall 1974), pp. 353–59.
Copyright 1974 by Newberry College. Reprinted with permission. Notes and references
in the original have been omitted in this reprint.

tween the narrations of Pip the boy and the commentary of Mr. Pip the man.

BLURRED NARRATIVE VOICES

In *A Separate Peace,* just as in *Great Expectations,* the shift from one narrative perspective to another is rarely obvious, and so the distinct jump that occurs on page 6 of Knowles's novel is the exception rather than the rule. But perhaps because it is so distinct, this example provides a clear illustration of the difference between the two narrative voices. Gene the man says, "The tree was not only stripped by the cold season, it seemed weary from age, enfeebled, dry," and nine lines later Gene the boy describes it as "tremendous, an irate, steely black steeple beside the river." Thereafter, the distinction between Gene's two narrative voices becomes more blurred, but it is, nevertheless, quite evident on such occasions as, for example, his description of the recognition that Finny's heart was "a den of lonely, selfish ambition." Indeed, for several pages Gene the boy attributes to Phineas characteristics that Gene the adult knows to be entirely absent from his personality, and it is only when the adult voice chooses to reveal to us the absolute falsity of these misconceptions that we discover, as Gene did himself, that Finny is incapable of harboring evil thoughts and feelings towards others. We are deliberately kept unaware of this recognition in order that we can share the intensity of Gene's misguided feelings, and so the boy's voice, which possesses the power of evoking the immediate actuality of an experience, is the exclusive narrator of this section of the story, handing over to the adult only when it becomes important that we understand correctly the significance of what has been happening.

In general, it is the boy's voice that narrates what happens in the novel, and the man's voice that interprets and conceptualizes these events. Sometimes, however, as in the incidents just discussed, the younger Gene also provides us with his interpretations of the actions, thoughts, and feelings of the characters, and when he does so we must be aware of the unreliability of his opinions. Usually, Knowles structures the narrative so that we are misled by the boy's misconceptions only for as long as seems necessary to express the actuality of his thoughts and feelings, and then the course of events, or the adult voice, reveals to us that this adolescent interpretation is false. For example, when Mrs. Patch-

Withers discovers at the headmaster's tea that Phineas is using the school tie as a belt, Gene says, "This time he wasn't going to get away with it. I could feel myself becoming unexpectedly excited at that." But then, of course, Finny does get away with it, and Gene tells us, "I felt a sudden stab of disappointment. That was because I just wanted to see some more excitement; that must have been it," a simplistic explanation that both the adult Gene and, retrospectively, the reader know to be an inadequate interpretation of a complex emotional reaction composed of admiration, envy, disappointment, and latent hatred. Again, when Gene comments on Finny's sensational performance in blitzball, it is clear that although he does not understand the nature of his own reaction, the reader and Gene's older self are meant to recognize it as another indication of his developing resentment of his roommate. "What difference did it make? It was just a game. It was good that Finny could shine at it. He could also shine at many other things, with people for instance, the others in our dormitory, the faculty; in fact, if you stopped to think about it, Finny could shine with everyone, he attracted everyone he met. I was glad of that too. Naturally. He was my roommate and my best friend." Moreover, the fact that this is the voice of the boy narrator is emphasized by the obvious difference in tone of the next paragraph, the narrator of which is clearly the adult: "Everyone has a moment in history which belongs to him. . . . For me, this moment—four years is a moment in history—was the war. The war was and is reality for me."

There are occasions, however, when the adult narrator does not later intervene to rectify young Gene's misconceptions, nor does the course of events serve to reveal the unreliability of his comments, and these are the instances when as readers we must be most careful not to accept Gene's interpretations without first scrutinizing them closely. This is particularly true of comments about Phineas. The short novel is primarily about Gene; but since Finny is the catalyst for Gene's developing personality, one must understand Phineas to understand the novel. With the exception of [critic] Peter Wolfe, commentators have been content to regard Finny as a static character, naive and romantic, who embodies all innocence, youthfulness, and purity, who cannot survive a collision with evil and violence, and who

therefore denies the reality of war and is inevitably crushed
by the adult, civilized, real, nasty world. This view accepts at
face value such comments of young Gene as that which begins Chapter 11: "I wanted to see Phineas, and Phineas only.
With him there was no conflict except between athletes,
something Greek-inspired and Olympian in which victory
would go to whoever was the strongest in body and heart.
This was the only conflict he had ever believed in." But Gene
is at this point suffering from the shock of Leper's madness,
and so, to counteract that violent reality, he idealizes
Phineas and invests him with a dignity and order, in contrast
to Leper's savage chaos, which he does not really possess.
And this should be evident from the next sentence in the
text: "When I got back I found him in the middle of a snowball fight." Nor is this even an ordered snowball fight, since
Finny organizes sides only so that he can turn on his original allies, doublecross his new allies, and so utterly con-
found all loyalties that "We ended the fight in the only way
possible; all of us turned on Phineas."

THE SIGNIFICANCE OF SPORTS

The snowball fight is important for two reasons. First, because it provides an example, other than the Winter Carnival,
of Phineas's celebration of winter—Peter Wolfe has written:
"By celebrating winter. . . . Phineas opts for life's harshness as
well as its joys." And second, because it exemplifies, as does
blitzball, Finny's attitude to sports. Gene tells us that his
friend's attitude is "'You always win at sports,'" and goes on to
add, "This 'you' was collective. Everyone always won at sports.
When you played a game you won, in the same way as when
you sat down to a meal you ate it. It inevitably and naturally
followed. Finny never permitted himself to realize that when
you won they lost. That would have destroyed the perfect
beauty which was sport. Nothing bad ever happened in
sports; they were the absolute good." But this reflection belongs to Gene the boy; it has been formed "As we drifted
through the summer," and may not, therefore, be reliable. In
fact, Finny's behavior at sports suggests that it is only partially
true. Neither in blitzball nor in the snowball fight is there anything tangible to be won or lost. There is no goal at which the
players can arrrive, nor can one team in any way defeat another since both activities are anarchic, based only on "reverses and deceptions," betrayal and treachery. Finny excels

at blitzball, but he is delighted to lose, in so far as anyone loses, in the snowball fight, just as "he couldn't ask for anything better" when Gene "jumped on top of him, my knees on his chest" on the way back from the fatal tree. We never see Finny engaged in a sport in which some are clearly victorious and some as clearly defeated. All his awards are for good sportsmanship rather than for being the victor in this sport or that. It therefore seems that, as far as Phineas is concerned, there is no goal in sports except the sheer enjoyment of the activity itself; just to participate is to win, and since everyone can participate no one need ever lose.

FINNY'S PERCEPTION OF REALITY

Nor is it only with reference to sports that we may see Finny to represent a denial of the need that most people feel to divide life into such opposing categories as win and lose, good and evil, fantasy and reality, truth and illusion, self and other. As [critic] Paul Witherington has pointed out, "His walk, his play, and even his body itself are described as a flow, a harmony within and without, a primitive attunement to natural cycles." Gene, on the other hand, describes his own life as "all those tangled strands which required the dexterity of a virtuoso to keep flowing"; but when, in his running, he suddenly finds his rhythm, breaks into the clear, arrives where Finny has always been, he says, "all entanglements were shed" as mind and body become one and he learns what it is to be an integrated personality. This above all is what Finny is, an integrated personality; just as "peace is indivisible," so is Phineas, and this means that he transcends the divisive categorizations that Gene, like most of us, attempts to impose on an indivisible universe. Not only is Finny frequently described in terms of flow, he is characterized as being possessed of extraordinary honesty, "simple, shocking self-acceptance," "uninterrupted, emphatic unity of strength," and great loyalty. All these attributes suggest that integrity, in the fullest meaning of that word, is the keystone of Phineas's character, for even his loyalty is comprehensive: "Finny had tremendous loyalty to the class, as he did to any group he belonged to, beginning with him and me and radiating outward past the limits of humanity towards spirits and clouds and the stars." And again, "He was too loyal to anything connected with himself—his roommate, his dormitory, his class, his school, outward in vastly expanded circles of loyalty until I couldn't imagine who would be excluded."

This loyalty, however, is only one expression of Finny's perception of the universe as an integrated and indivisible unity. From this perception comes his desire to celebrate winter as well as summer; his ability, after his accident, to think of Gene "as an extension of himself," and to transfer to him the athletic abilities that he is now incapable of exercising; his idea that "when they discovered the circle"—the universal symbol of completeness, wholeness, integrity— "they created sports"; his assertion that "when you really love something then it loves you back, in whatever way it has to love"; and his realization that war is a violation of sanity. Leper's madness is a confirmation of Finny's assertion that "the whole world is on a Funny Farm now" because the world is engaged in breaking in pieces the natural integrity of life, and Finny is able to recognize this because he has fallen victim to that "something ignorant in the human heart" which has "broken his harmonious and natural unity." Indeed, it is perhaps precisely because he knows what war is really like that Finny denies its existence, both to protect his own sanity—Leper goes mad when he meets the inverted disorder that is war—and to shelter his friends for as long as possible from its violent ravages. Nor is this possibility contradicted by Finny's revelation that he has all along been attempting to enlist in some branch, any branch, of the service. His intense loyalty compels him to do so, but Gene is, of course, absolutely correct in his recognition that this loyalty could never be limited only to Phineas's allies, but would naturally extend to the enemy as well.

FINNY'S CONTRADICTIONS

For much of the novel Gene seems to regard Finny's personality as full of contradictions: "a student who combined a calm ignorance of the rules with a winning urge to be good, who seemed to love the school truly and deeply, and never more than when he was breaking the regulations, a model boy who was most comfortable in the truant's corner." But Gene's development throughout the course of the novel includes a gradual acquisition of understanding which culminates in his recognition of Phineas's "way of sizing up the world with erratic and entirely personal reservations, letting its rocklike facts sift through and be accepted only a little at a time, only as much as he could assimilate without a sense of chaos and loss." Finny realizes that facts are not everything, and that to attempt to reduce reality to a collection of facts, to accept facts as equivalent to reality, as Brinker Hadley does, is to accept a chaotic part in place of an ordered whole and hence to suffer "a sense of chaos and loss." Phineas may often seem to contradict himself, but to such an accusation there is [Walt] Whitman's reply:

> Do I contradict myself?
> Very well then I contradict myself,
> (I am large, I contain multitudes).
>
> "Song of Myself," 51; 1324

It need not necessarily be the case, therefore, that Finny represents a way of looking at life that is so limited, so idealistic, so ignorant of actuality, that contact with reality inevitably shatters it. Instead, he is perhaps possessed of a transcendent clarity of perception that is capable of taking a larger view of life than is normal, and dies only because he is eventually outgunned by the forces that limit, reduce, and fragment the comprehensive integrity of existence.

It is, however, only possible to entertain such a view of Phineas's character and role in the novel if one first recognizes that some of the interpretations that we have of his actions, his feelings, and his thoughts derive from the unreliable commentary of Gene the boy. In order to overcome the limitations of conventional first-person narration, Knowles has divided the narrator's function between two versions of the same person, and there are, as one would expect, considerable differences in perception and understanding between the seventeen-year-old boy who conveys the immediacy of the experiences he narrates and the thirty-two-year-old man whose interpretations of those experiences provide the basis for our understanding of the novella. It is important, therefore, that when the boy narrator does comment on the significance of the action, we exercise greater than usual skepticism before we accept the validity of his opinions.

Irony

Walter R. McDonald

According to Walter R. McDonald, John Knowles uses irony as a technique in *A Separate Peace;* not only does irony guide character and plot, it also provides a tool with which to explore thematic material, especially the human potential for evil. McDonald finds the novel's conclusion particularly ironic: Gene rationalizes that some blind, ignorant impulse caused his actions and in the end proclaims that he has killed his enemy—his self-ignorance. In reality, Gene remains shackled in defense mechanisms, clearly unable, according to McDonald, to achieve self-awareness. McDonald is Paul Whitfield Horn Professor of English and director of the creative writing program at Texas Techical University. He contributed this essay to the *Iowa English Bulletin Yearbook.*

Unlike so many contemporary open-ended novels, John Knowles' popular story *A Separate Peace* appears to end with its main figure as resolved and self-aware as a hero in a [Charles] Dickens' tale. Yet there is in Gene Forrester's adjustment—his separate peace with his own conscience—an essential lie, or half-truth, or, better, a low-keyed irony. Irony, in fact, is the subtle but controlling technique that functions in the entire novel, in terms of characterization, development of episode, and theme.

The protagonist, Gene Forrester, having concluded that he jounced the tree limb and ruined his friend Phineas simply because of "something ignorant in the human heart," returns to Devon years later and, still believing this motive, discovers that the fateful tree has shrunk and that he himself has matured, has learned, has achieved "growth and harmony" by putting the events of his life in proper perspective. Ironically, however, Gene Forrester, who thinks he has learned so much about himself, has only begun to learn; he is, in fact, ignorant in his self-knowledge.

Reprinted from Walter R. McDonald, "Heroes Never Learn: Irony in *A Separate Peace,*" *Iowa English Bulletin Yearbook*, vol. 22 (1972), pp. 33–36, by permission of the Iowa Council Teachers of English and Language Arts.

The easy irony that the school's weakest and best scholars, Phineas and Gene, are roommates sets up the story's inevitable conflict. They are, ironically enough, exactly even in height, as Phineas pointedly reminds Gene ("Never say you are five feet nine when you are five feet eight and a half"), thus touching off their competition. And however much Gene denies it at the end, the aggressive sense of competition is there. Early in the story when Phineas wears his school tie as a belt, Gene feels a "sudden stab of disappointment" when Phineas gets away with it, unpunished. It is another easy irony, with obvious self-delusion, when Gene rationalizes his malicious disappointment as simply that he "just wanted to see some more excitement; that must have been it." From the beginning, Gene refuses to recognize that there is malice in his own heart.

A BLIND IMPULSE

Finny is no different after his second fall: unable to admit that Gene has injured him intentionally, he cries out, "It was just some kind of blind impulse you had in the tree there, you didn't know what you were doing." And gratefully, Gene responds, "Yes, yes, that was it. Oh that was it."

But was that it? Was it just a blind impulse? Finny grasps at it, desperately seeking a defense against the truth: "Something just seized you. It wasn't anything you really felt against me, it wasn't some kind of hate you've felt all along. It wasn't anything personal." And Gene agrees, expressing what he considers the essential "truth" that he has learned: "It was just some ignorance inside me, some crazy thing inside me, something blind, that's all it was." Convinced of this "truth," Gene expands it to explain how wars come about (indeed, we are to see the entire story of Devon as a microcosm of World War II, or of all wars). As Gene says, "It seemed clear that wars were not made by generations and their special stupidities, but that wars were made instead by something ignorant in the human heart."

HUMAN EVIL

If that were all there is to the book, Knowles' theme would be bleakly evident, a hopeless nihilism, with generations forever doomed to ignorantly repeat the evils of the past, never learning from them. But there is more to the story, I believe; Knowles raises deeper, more significant questions about human evil. The answers to these questions remain hidden to Gene throughout the story, limited as he is by his own defense mechanisms. The cause of Finny's fall is not ignorance, not a blindness that just suddenly appears; rather, it is the result of a malice that has been growing in Gene all along—a rivalry, a jealousy, a spite that builds in Gene before the fateful jump.

But Gene is an artful dodger; and the skimming reader may be lulled by Gene's rationalization into forgetting about all this hate, concluding with Gene and Finny that it was after all merely some blind ignorant impulse, and nothing personal. Knowles himself says that even the thirty-three-year-old Gene Forrester, when he returns to Devon after the war, still believes the last two paragraphs of the book—that is, that it was just blind ignorance that had made him jounce Finny off the limb and that only Finny was never afraid.

[Joseph] Conrad's Lord Jim may puzzle over his moment of failure on the *Patna* ("I jumped," Jim says, "it seemed"). But we can see too clearly into Gene Forrester's heart shortly before he jounces the limb: thinking, Gene discovers that Finny "had never been jealous of me for a second. Now I knew that there never was and never could have been any rivalry between us. I was not of the same quality as he. *I couldn't stand this*" [(emphasis added).] Two paragraphs later, he jounces the limb—consciously innocent, yes; morally culpable, maybe not; but explicably responsible, most certainly. Athletes call this process "psyching" themselves up, getting mentally ready—such as a weight lifter who takes seconds, even minutes, to concentrate. Then, once engaged, he reacts spontaneously. Cybernetics is the more technical term, or psychocybernetics, as popularized by Dr. Maxwell Maltz.

So when Finny cries that it was not some hate Gene had been feeling all along, he touches the truth, but ironically, for it is a felt, but unfelt hostility that Gene has programmed in himself, thus causing his knees to bend mechanically—"like a piston," as Leper says. Speaking at the Air Force Academy in 1970 Knowles referred to it as a "seizure."

But it is not some mysterious blind impulse we can do nothing about, as Gene with Finny's urging comes to believe. Finny of course, not Gene, is the prime mover behind the false belief. Earlier, Gene has tried to confess: "I jounced the limb . . . I deliberately jounced the limb so you would fall off." But of course he has not "deliberately," consciously jounced the limb, and his confession is too crude, itself only a distorted half-truth, at which Finny recoils, "Of course you didn't. . . . Go away. I'm tired and you make me sick."

Finny cannot even entertain the idea that Gene would want to hurt him. Later, almost believing his own fantasy, Finny claims during the second trial scene that Gene was on the ground when the event occurred. Gratefully, Gene agrees, knowing better. But Finny has concocted too crude a fantasy as his defense, and he cannot keep faith in it, but stalks out in anger and terror when Leper begins telling his version of fact. Finally, lying defeated in the infirmary, Phineas comes up with "blind instinct" as the excuse for Gene's action, and Gene grasps at it, also, crying, "Yes, yes." "Thus conscience doth make cowards of us all."

Thematically, the story concerns Phineas as innocence personified, innocence that must be broken, as Knowles told the Air Force Academy cadets. Leper remarks that the war is "like a test . . . and only the . . . people who've been evolving the right way survive." Gene survives by making his accommodation to brutal truth, by bending with the truth rather than resisting and being broken by it. The others at Devon, also, though Gene says they are "broken," have actually evolved with various defense mechanisms which "parry the menace" they see. Only Finny and Leper refuse and refuse again to look at life, until seeing it, they cry with Kurtz "the horror, the horror"; without adequate defenses, they are destroyed.

THE SHOCK OF RECOGNITION

At the end Gene claims that "Only Phineas never was afraid. . . . Other people experienced this fearful shock somewhere, this sighting of the enemy." But the fact is that Finny does *not* survive; thematically, it *is* this fearful shock of recognition that kills him. Since Finny cannot bear the idea that his friend has within him a hatred capable of such destruction, he, so innocent that he breaks a school swimming record in private but will not do so in public competition, constructs "at infinite cost" to himself an inadequate Maginot Line against his real enemy, the brutalizing effect of life's competitive spirit.

Ironically, Phineas himself has named such an act of denial the "Lepellier refusal." Here, too, irony patterns the book, as Leper's refusals foreshadow Finny's. First, Leper refuses to jump; he refuses to engage in the conflict of blitzball (that wonderfully ironic game, invented by Finny, of playing at

It was as though a wave, a very large wave, were gathering
force in the distance and moving toward me. There was a far-
off rumbling coming nearer; letters, then more letters, began
to arrive from readers; then teachers took the book up by the
thousands, and the sales climbed and climbed. . . .

And how did all this feel, as it happened, the prizes and the
praise and the movie and the admiration of great numbers of
young people?

It was what the book deserved. I say what the book deserved, because it did tend to acquire a destiny apart from
mine, and I feel about it the way a parent with a rather
workaday existence must feel when he finds he has produced
a world-beating child: a slight sense of wonder, pride, and a
certain detachment.

As more and more people read it and as it was taught over
and over in schools, *A Separate Peace* became public property.
People began talking proprietarily about it, and if I murmured
a dissent as to their view of my work, they tended to look
askance and then go on explaining what it was *really* all
about.

John Knowles, "My Separate Peace," *Esquire*, March 1985.

war); he refuses to shovel snow from the railroad tracks to aid
the war effort; and finally, of course, after ironically being the
first of his class to enlist, he refuses the horror of army life and
goes psychotic.

Although apparently the opposite of Leper, Finny follows
the pattern: he refuses to conform to the school's rules; he refuses to let his swimming record be reported for competition;
he refuses even the idea that there is a war going on (though
he writes secretively, desperately to every branch of service to
enlist). He refuses Gene's first confession of guilt; and finally,
at the trial, he refuses to listen to Leper's testimony about
Gene's guilt and brings on himself the fall down the hard
marble stairs that leads to his death.

The novel's grisly irony if Gene's claim, "I killed my enemy
there" at the school (the enemy being "self-ignorance").
Finny, as the epitome of this "self-ignorance" and child-like

innocence, must be broken, thematically, for Gene to begin maturing, making a horrible underlying pun of Gene's confession, "I killed my enemy [(Finny)] there."

Ironically, though, he has not killed his personal self-ignorance and has not fully evolved. At the Air Force Academy, Knowles described Gene's jouncing of the limb as a "seizure, but which nevertheless came out of himself, and for which he was responsible." Since Gene believes it was an impulse, he therefore believes a half-truth. With ambivalence, he did hate Finny, was spiteful; and Finny himself was not a perfect Greek god, but a frightened prep school boy not daring to face the truth and who was therefore even more self-ignorant than Gene, who at least survives.

Gene concludes at the end that Phineas possessed "a serene capacity for affection which saved him." But the irony which Gene has not yet realized at all is that Finny's Maginot Line of naive affection, blind to the dangerous ambivalence within man, is exactly that which destroys him. To deliver one's self from evil as Finny does leads to one's own destruction, for reality is ignored; to deliver one's self from evil as Gene does is to blind one's conscience and thus render more evil. The epiphany, then, the valuable insight of the ordeal, is the reader's more than Gene's; and Gene's discovery—which is the book's apparent conclusion—is only a half-truth, necessarily ironic.

CHAPTER 3

Important Themes in *A Separate Peace*

Moral Ambiguity

Paul Witherington

A Separate Peace is often read as an allegory of
man's fall from innocence: Finny falls physically
without sin and Gene falls spiritually without any
physical harm. In the following essay, Paul Witherington takes issue with this interpretation asserting
that the novel does not express a rigid code of good
and evil but rather an ambiguous moral atmosphere.
People and their emotions are complex. Thus, Finny
is not spiritually pure and wholly benevolent as
some critics have suggested; likewise, Gene is not
spiritually depraved or devoid of redeeming qualities. Ultimately, Gene finds peace by accepting the
inevitable ambiguities of human nature. Witherington taught at the University of the Pacific in Stockton,
California.

The development and resolution of tensions between Gene
and Finny provide the well-balanced structure of *A Separate
Peace*, as several critics have noted. What has not been ap-
preciated, however, is the ambiguity of the boys' conflict in
its several phases, an ambiguity expressed in both character
and symbol. The story is not a simple allegory of man's fortunate or unfortunate fall from innocence, or even an extension of that theological debate to the process of growing up,
though both of these arguments are in the novel. Rather,
Knowles is investigating patterns of society as a whole, patterns consisting of ambiguous tensions between rigidity and
flexibility, involvement and isolation, and magic and art. To
understand the necessity of a broader interpretation of the
novel than has been generally given, one must see that for
Knowles opposite emotions and forces often only seem to
face or move in contrary directions.

The relationship between Finny and Gene is said to be
one of primitive innocence confronted with and eventually

From Paul Witherington, "*A Separate Peace:* A Study in Structural Ambiguity," *English
Journal*, vol. 54 (1965), pp. 795–800. Copyright 1965 by the National Council of Teachers of English. Reprinted with permission. Notes and references in the original have
been omitted in this reprint.

destroyed by the necessities of civilization. Natural, noble Finny, another of the durable procession of American Adams, is maimed and hounded out of Eden by the hatred he is finally forced to see in his best friend, Gene. On the other hand, Gene's emerging recognition of his guilt in Finny's fall from the tree signals his passage from childhood's innocent play to the responsible ethical concerns of adulthood. Phrased socially rather than theologically, there is a movement toward acceptance of the outside world—that of World War II—and corresponding acceptance of the fact that wars occur not only between nations but between individuals, sometimes even friends, and that the blame in either case can be traced to lack of understanding, an ignorance in the human heart.

THE NATURE OF SUFFERING

One difficulty in such interpretations is that Knowles resists defining innocence and evil and their interaction in simplified, allegoric terms. If there are parallels to Eden, they must surely be ironic, for Finny falls physically without sin whereas Gene falls spiritually without any recognizable physical discomfort. Finny's fall (he falls twice, actually, once from the tree and once on the steps at Devon) seems to represent an awareness of evil that is incompatible with his basic assumptions about unity and goodness; his gradual acceptance of Gene's hostility is accompanied by a physical decline which is strongest at the moments of greatest disillusion. But this awareness of evil remains merely physical in Finny. When asked how he knows that World War II is not real, he says, "Because I've suffered." It appears that nothing is learned after all, that Finny never really understands the world around him. . . . Gene, on the other hand, seems to endure and even to thrive on his knowledge of evil. His metaphysical fall is, after all, painless, for unlike Claggart in Melville's allegory of good and evil, *Billy Budd,* Gene is untouched by the thrust of mistreated innocence; his moments of mental anguish seem strangely inadequate when compared to those of his classmate, Leper. Greek drama develops in Western literature the notion of suffering as a means to understanding, and American literature is full of innocents who fall from purity only to gain a much more valuable wisdom, but the irony in Knowles is that the sufferer does not understand the nature or purpose of his suffering, and the one who does not suffer both understands and prospers. The world of *A Separate Peace* is not the world of Hawthorne but the inverted, shifting mythos of Kafka, for example, the ambiguous moral atmosphere of "In the Penal Colony."

Apparently complicating matters still further is Finny's announcement near the end of the novel that he has really known there was a war all the time, that his pretending otherwise was his defense against being unable to go to war with his friends. Knowles may have gotten himself into a structural dilemma here; what seems at first in Finny a genuine misconception of human character, a metaphysical innocence, has become a rationalization, the suppression of an unpleasant fact; illusion becomes delusion, and the reader may conclude that Knowles has lost control of his character, that what started as a semiabstract personification of innocence has come to life as a fully realized character who says that, after all, the grapes really were sour.

COMPLEX CHARACTERS

The answer to these problems is that Finny is no more of a spiritually pure being than Gene is a spiritually depraved being. Both boys project their inadequacies onto others; Gene's transfer of his own hostility onto Finny is balanced by Finny's notion that wars are contrived by "fat old men" who profit from wartime economy. Moreover, Finny is a breaker of rules, not incidentally but systematically. Gene says, of Devon's rigid system of discipline, "If you broke the rules, then they broke you." Finny's anarchy, however, gives rise to a set of rules just as rigid as the school's and just as imperative; Gene describes Finny's pressure for misbehavior metaphorically: "Like a police car squeezing me to the side of the road, he directed me unwillingly toward the gym and the river." Finny's effort to entice Gene from his studies appears just as conscious as Gene's movement of the tree limb causing Finny's fall.

There is something almost diabolical about Finny's "innocence." His power over people is uncanny; Gene describes it as hypnotic, and it consists of inducing others temporarily to suspend their practical, logical systems of belief to follow his non-logical argument, acted out either verbally or on the playing fields. The answers he gives in class are "often not right but could rarely be branded as wrong," for they presuppose a world in which ordinary standards of judgment are impossible. Finny's pranks themselves—skipping classes and meals, wearing the school tie as a belt, playing poker in the dorm—are actually serious offenses only within the disciplinary framework of a prep school. The audacity is his defense of them which is always disconcerting because it is never relevant, or sometimes too relevant, as when he is being frank about a normally touchy subject. Finny's simplicity, by its very rarity, tends to shock and to threaten the established order of things, to throw ordinary people off balance.

Further ambiguity exists in the imagery of flow which Knowles uses to describe Finny's harmony with others and with his environment. Friendship to Finny is a harmony of equal tensions and movements. Like his idea that everybody always wins at sports, this notion of reciprocal benevolence naively presupposes a level of human interaction superior not only to individual selfishness but also to pressures and events of the actual world. "When you really love something, then it loves you back," he tells Gene, but when Finny confesses his feelings for Gene on the beach, Gene is too embarrassed to answer. Finny cannot understand why people build walls between what they feel and what they let others know they feel; his benevolence, a two-way avenue between friends, is his reason for being. His walk, his play and even his body itself are described as a flow, a harmony within and without, a primitive attunement to natural cycles. The world of graduation, the draft, and adult necessity is oriented differently, however, and Finny's rhythm is broken in his fall into the civilized world: "There was an interruption, brief as a drum beat, in the continuous flow of his walk, as though with each step he forgot for a split-second where he was going." After Finny's second fall, on the stairs, he dies when bone marrow gets in the bloodstream and stops his heart.

Yet Knowles is careful not to oversimplify nor to sentimentalize Finny's stopped flow, the heart ruptured by a violent world. Like the Devon River, that clear, innocent center of summer fun in which the boys play their last summer of childhood, Finny is shut off from natural progress, damned into isolation and perpetual youth. Below the dam the Naguamsett River, center of winter activity and symbolic setting of Gene's "baptism" into the world of adulthood, is "ugly, saline, fringed with marsh, mud and seaweed," but it does flow into the world-encircling sea to be influenced by the Gulf Stream, the Polar Ice Cap, and the moon; like Gene it, eventually, after some difficulty, involves itself in world movements. The Devon and Finny are relics of some earlier, less complex era, self-sufficient but out of the flow of time, able to give rise and even direction to the stream of mankind, but themselves unable to follow into a mature involvement. There is irony in the fact that Gene's rigid, West Point stride endures, whereas Finny's graceful body breaks so easily; of course Finny risks much more, for his position is supported precariously by shaky illusions. Like Billy Budd's stutter which seems aggravated in the moments when he confronts evil in the world and has no adequate language to express his feelings about it, Finny's flawed flow steadily becomes worse with each new awareness of the hate around him.

Finally, love and hate are themselves ambiguous in *A Separate Peace*, from Gene's first suspicions of an undercurrent of rivalry till the time in the army when he wonders if the "enemy" he killed at Devon was really an enemy at all. Gene is never sure of his relationship with Finny because he—like the reader who sees the action through Gene's eyes—is never sure what Finny represents, whether he is a well-meaning friend who simply resists growing up, a pernicious fraud acting out of spite, or a neurotic who builds protective illusions.

THE HUMAN CONDITION

Ambiguity, then, seems to be Knowles' method of showing that people and their emotions must be treated as complex rather than as simple. Good and evil, love and hatred, involvement and isolation, self and selflessness are not always clearly defined nor their values constant. Part of growing up is the recognition that the human condition is a dappled one, that the wrong we feel in things is often only some pattern erected by fear and ignorance, some rigidity that divides life into lifeless compartments. It remains to show how these patterns are fashioned in the novel and what their effects are on the central characters.

All the boys at Devon build barriers against the outside world; "Maginot Lines" Knowles calls them to emphasize their obsolescence and vulnerability. Leper, Devon's introverted biology student, hunts beaver far up the Devon River, detached and unconcerned, masking fear with a mechanistic approach to life symbolized by his movements on skiis, those of a "homemade piston engine." His opposite type is Brinker, the class leader, too busy arranging and presiding over school activities to be frightened of the world outside. Like his father, who exploited service in World War I for its social advantages, Brinker treats war as a necessary but inefficient initiation into community leadership, summing it up in his "shortest war poem": "The war/is a bore." Neither case is meant to be typical, for Knowles is concerned with the poles of experience, not its midsection. Leper shows the fallacy of hiding so far from society that the return is a threat to sanity; the fantasy world he fashions turns into a nightmare in boot camp where he begins to have hallucinations in which things are turned "inside out." Brinker is too close to society to preserve any self-identity or to see others as real, separate people, and he is submerged in a kind of public fantasy. The major patterns, of course, are those described in Finny and Gene, ways of approaching the problems posed by growing up and adjusting to civilization, patterns for the two boys respectively of magic and naturalism.

SHIELDS AGAINST REALITY

For Finny, life is a continuous effort to control reality by creating comfortable myths about it. War is only make-believe on the fields and rivers of Devon: a game resembling football and soccer is invented and named, for its speed and devastating unpredictability, "blitzball"; snowball fights are staged as military operations; the tree hanging over the Devon River is a torpedoed ship that must be evacuated. But these games which at first seem to have the practical function of preparing boys mentally and physically for war actually become shields against reality, ways of sugarcoating the externals of war by making its participants invulnerable, like playful Olympian deities. Finny is unable to distinguish between playing and fighting, the forms of which seem similar within his romantic, naive frame of reference. Like his theory of reciprocal benevolence, his theory of games is based on the assumption that what *should be* true *can be* once the proper pattern is erected. It is true that Finny is a superb athlete who usually wins any physical contest, and it is also true that Finny often defines winning and losing—the rules of the game itself—during play, but the real basis for Finny's notion that everybody always wins at sports is his idea that the game consists in finding a

proper method of play which then makes its outcome irrele-
vant. His rigidity in this respect is most apparent in a game he
plays badly, poker. Following a plan that ought to win, Finny
ignores the fact that he actually never does, even when the
game is his own weird invention, like a child who asks and
keeps asking a question, learning the language by which to
frame it and seeming not to hear the answer that is given.

Finny appears essential to Devon's organized defense
against war, not only because he directs the boys' last peaceful
summer of play and infuses it with ideals of love and equal interaction, but because he seems to have the power to sustain
this idyllic atmosphere beyond its natural limits. Described by
Gene, Finny is a primitive, god-like priest celebrating the essential unity and indestructibility of man and nature and me-
diating between the two: "Phineas in exaltation, balancing on
one foot on the prow of a canoe like a river god, his raised
arms invoking the air to support him, face transfigured, body
a complex set of balances and compensations, each muscle
aligned in perfection with all the others to maintain the
supreme fantasy of achievement, his skin glowing from im-
mersions, his whole body hanging between river and sky as
though he had transcended gravity and might by gently pushing upward with his foot glide a little way higher and remain
suspended in space, encompassing all the glory of the summer
and offering it to the sky." Even after he falls from the tree,
Finny preserves this function as priest. His broken body makes
winter seem inevitable but only temporary, and his creation of
the winter carnival by fiat ["And because it was Finny's idea, it
happened as he said"] is an act of magic designed to recreate
the harmony of summer. The ritual is begun by burning the
Iliad, not so much as a protest against war as a magical attempt to destroy war by destroying an early, typical account of
it. Standing on a table at the ceremonies, hopping about on his
one good leg in protest against war and deformity, Finny tries
to represent life as he feels it should be; the others, intoxicated
with their desire for earlier, less demanding forms of existence, allow Finny to lead them in this "choreography of
peace," suggesting Hart Crane's line in *The Bridge:* "Lie to us–
–dance us back the tribal morn."

FINNY'S DOWNFALL

In Finny's universe all things are possible as long as the bul-
wark of illusion holds; as long as Finny can believe each

morning, for example, that his leg has overnight been miraculously healed, there is evidence for all magic, not only his but that of a sympathetic universe. When reality does not meet his expectations, though, he is gradually forced into a defensive position. At Gene's "trial" by fellow students, Finny testifies that he believed the tree itself shook him out and jumbled him to the ground. This is more than a defense of Gene, just as the "trial" is more than Gene's; it is Finny's defense of himself, of his notions of reciprocal benevolence and of the inner harmony of all things, and of that supernatural world which sustains these illusions. The evidence convicts him as well as Gene, but—as his second fall shows—Finny cannot adapt to the fact of a Darwinian universe, a world where there are no absolute principles, but only the reality met in experience. The danger of building unsupportable myths like Finny's is shown in Knowles' second novel *Morning in Antibes* (1962); Nick, the central character, in a state of agony at losing his own hold on reality, "spontaneously" composes a poem illustrating his condition:

> The tightrope walker is tired
> Because he must always lean forward
> To weave the rope
> (*Morning in Antibes*)

The fall comes—as in so many movie cartoons—not when one does the impossible, but when one realizes that he is doing what in fact is impossible. Finny dies when he realizes he has had no magic, that he can no longer, as Knowles puts it, exist "primarily in space." The other boys are propelled forward into the real world by the force of Finny's violent death, for spring inexorably comes in spite of his physical decay, and the correspondence between the priest and the object of his religion is broken.

Finny's imagination moves always from war to play, first grasping the game as a simile for war and then—when the thought of training for something which he cannot use becomes unendurable—playing the game as a substitute for war. The imaginations of the other boys move in opposite directions, from play to war, for that is the way of growing up, recognizing that the patterns of childhood are masks behind which stand the real patterns of life. One day at Devon these different imaginations, facing opposite directions, reach a high moment of dramatic tension in a mock snow war that prefigures Finny's death: "We ended the fight in the only way possible; all of us turned on Phineas. Slowly, with a steadily widening grin, he was driven down beneath a blizzard of snowballs."

Afterwards on the way back to the gym, Finny remarks that it was a good, funny fight. Gene does not answer; he has for some time had conscious premonitions about things to come, about a turned-inside-out situation where games become real wars: "I didn't trust myself in them, and I didn't trust anyone else. It was as though football players were really bent on crushing the life out of each other, as though boxers were in combat to the death, as though even a tennis ball might turn into a bullet." This is a prelude to the awareness that world wars are but expansions of individual hatred and ignorance and therefore anticlimactic to the anguish of growing up. For Gene the war with Germany and Japan is a simile for his experiences at Devon, less intense because less personal.

THE CONSCIOUSNESS OF AMBIGUITY

The ability to see patterns between world wars and personal wars and between friendly and hostile conflict is to see at once the horrible depravity and the irony of the world where varying and even conflicting experiences often take on the same form. This consciousness of ambiguity, this appreciation of the variety and relativity of human experience, is what Gene learns. His movement, in short, is not toward the primitive, magical effort to control reality in the sense of making it fit preconceived ideas but toward the naturalistic effort to understand reality by relating it to forms of personal experience. As the patterns of experience are realized, they take on meaning, and this meaning itself is a kind of control, not that of the magician but of the artist who finds order and harmony in the structure of things rather than in categorical moral imperatives.

Rejecting Finny's magical view promotes in Gene a new awareness of self and a new self-responsibility. As the compulsive rituals of Finny give way to Gene's nonprescriptive view, and myth is conceived as serving experience rather than dictating it, Gene separates himself from his environment and recognizes in himself the capabilities for idealism and hatred he had formerly projected on the outside world. This emancipation is represented symbolically in Gene's changing relationship with Finny. At first he thinks of himself, rather guiltily, as an extension of Finny, but after becoming an athlete in his own right he sees Finny as smaller, both relatively and absolutely, like memories from childhood, like the tree at Devon which seemed "high as a beanstalk" and yet is scarcely recognizable years later. Finally Gene thinks of himself as including Finny ("Phineasfilled"), and this indicates his maturity: preserving the myth associated with Finny but only so it can serve him as it serves the artist, as a metaphor for experience.

GENE'S SEPARATE PEACE

Finny tries to construct a separate peace by explaining away the war as a fraud or by ignoring its content of violence, and Knowles' message is, of course, that this is impossible. Much as Finny's ideal world of changelessness, irresponsibility, and illusion is desirable—and Knowles does present it as desirable—one must eventually abandon it for the world of possibility. Gene's final comment, made on his return to Devon years after the major action of the novel, is the key to what he has learned from the tragedy of Finny: "Nothing endures, not a tree, not love, not even a death by violence. Changed, I headed back through the mud. I was drenched; anybody could see it was time to come in out of the rain." Gene frees himself from fear not by hiding from war and the ambiguities of the human heart, not by building barriers between youth and age, but by accepting the inevitability of change and loss. The act of coming in out of the rain, that ancient criterion distinguishing the idealist from the realist, represents the peace Gene finds, the treaty established between what the world should be and what it really is.

Levels of Meaning

Milton P. Foster

In this analysis, Milton P. Foster argues that John
Knowles presents many layers of meaning that coa-
lesce into a complex, meaningful story. At the narrative level is the carefully crafted story of the friendship
between Gene and Finny. Other levels of meaning
concern fear and hatred, sin and forgiveness, war and
peace, and also the timeless theme of a good man—
Finny—at odds with a corrupt world. In each case,
these levels of meaning overlap and support the most
important theme in *A Separate Peace*—man's search
for self-knowledge. Foster was a professor of English
at Eastern Michigan University.

Soon after they are introduced to the novel as a serious work
of art, students should learn the concept of levels of meaning
in fiction. The teacher can demonstrate that a well made
novel has both unity and complexity; he can point out that a
novel has a unifying idea, and then he can show that this idea
is developed through many levels of meaning. *A Separate
Peace* by John Knowles is an excellent novel for illustrating
these qualities. On the surface level *A Separate Peace* is the
story of a prep-school friendship that ends tragically. If this
were all there is to the novel it would still be a noteworthy
achievement. The friendship between Gene Forrester and
Phineas is pictured with such skill and unsentimental realism
that it is completely believable. It corresponds with experience. In addition, the somber outcome of the story gives the
reader a deeply moving experience. The novel can be thoroughly enjoyed on this strictly narrative level, but fortunately
there is much more to it than this.

Beneath the surface *A Separate Peace* also provides us
with a study of fear and the hate that results from fear. Early
in the novel when we are just becoming acquainted with
Gene Forrester, through whose consciousness the story is

Reprinted from Milton P. Foster, "Levels of Meaning in *A Separate Peace*," *English
Record*, vol. 18 (April 1968), pp. 34–40 with permission.

revealed, the emotion of fear is introduced. As Gene revisits his school fifteen years after the time of the story, he tells us he could feel again in the old, familiar buildings the "well known fear" that he had felt there in his senior year, even though he had escaped from that fear since graduation. One place on campus that was especially fearful to Gene was a large tree. The tree was fearful because it was there that Finny had pressured Gene to make the dangerous jump into the Devon River night after night during the summer session of 1942, and it was even more fearful because it was there that Gene was surprised by the sudden burst of hate in himself that caused him to make Finny fall from the tree and break his leg. Prior to that fall Gene had reluctantly come to the conclusion that his best friend Finny was no friend at all, that Finny had been challenging him to nightly tree jumps and other dangerous and time-consuming exploits only to prevent Gene from being the school's top student academically, rivaling Finny, who was the school's best athlete. Gene had come to realize before the incident at the tree that he was judging Finny unfairly and that Finny was after all a true best friend, but while they were both standing on the tree, some unexpected evil force inside Gene made him shake Finny off the tree. This force, the author implies, was an unconscious hatred, a hatred engendered by fear— Gene's irrational fear of Finny's domination over him. Through this incident John Knowles has reminded us of the sad truth about human nature that we hate because we fear.

SIN AND FORGIVENESS

A third level of meaning in the novel concerns sin and forgiveness. The outward form of the sin is Gene's betrayal of Finny by making him fall from the tree. The real meaning of this sinful act, as is true of all sinful acts, is separation. As we are told the details of the almost ideal friendship between Gene and Finny in the first part of the novel, we gradually see that Gene and Finny are almost one person. They are the same height and almost the same weight, they are roommates, they wear each other's clothes, they collaborate instinctively in breaking the rules of Devon School, they say their silent prayers together before going to sleep, they are the only boys daring enough to jump from the tree, and they do this together. One excels in mind; the other in body. Gene breaks this nearly perfect unity when he resents Finny's persuasive leadership, and he makes the gulf greater when he gives in to the ugly suspicion that Finny is trying to destroy his scholastic record. This separation is the state of sin that the novel explores. It leads to Finny's fall from the tree, which, as a spiritual fall, is just as serious a fall for Gene, his *alter ego.* Finny is physically crippled afterwards. Gene is spiritually crippled, or maimed, to use the word John Knowles uses in the Quackenbush incident a little later in the novel.

Knowles does not stop with giving us an understanding of the essence of sin. Through the remarkable character of Finny we also gain an understanding of the desired sequel to sin—forgiveness. When Gene visits Finny, now an invalid, in his Boston home before the fall session begins and tells him that he deliberately jounced him off the limb, Finny flatly rejects the idea. Later in the fall term when Finny comes back late to school, he is delighted to be Gene's room-mate again. When he hears that Gene might enlist in the armed forces, he is shocked and depressed. Seeing this re-action, Gene in amazement thinks to himself, "He needed me. I was the least trustworthy person he had ever met. I knew that; he knew or should know that too. I had even told him. I had told him. But there was no mistaking the shield of remoteness in his face and voice. He wanted me around."

This reconciliation leads to an even closer unity of Gene and Finny than before the fall. Finny is filled with joy when Gene drops his plans to enlist. The two experience again for a while the special peace they had enjoyed during the summer session. With Gene tutoring Finny in studies and Finny tutor-ing Gene in sports, Gene accomplishes amazing physical feats, and Finny almost becomes a good student. Their har-mony, however, is suddenly shattered when their friend, Brinker Hadley, forces them to attend a mock investigation into Finny's accident, at which Gene's guilt is brought to light. Finny cannot reject the truth this time, and rushing out of the room in a rage with his leg still in a cast, he falls down a mar-ble stairway and breaks his leg again. But in the hospital the next day he finds the power in himself to overcome hatred and forgive Gene. This forgiveness purifies Gene's spirit so that when the time comes he can enter the war undefiled: "I had no qualms at all; in fact I could feel now the gathering, glowing sense of sureness in the face of it. I was ready for the war, now that I no longer had any hatred to contribute to it. My fury was gone, I felt it gone, dried up at the source, withered and lifeless. Phineas had absorbed it and taken it with him, and I was rid of it forever." Christ-like, with his body broken for Gene, Finny loves, forgives, and helps to make whole the man who has betrayed him. E.M. Forster has said that *A Separate Peace* reminds him of the *Philoctetes* of Sophocles. Perhaps he saw in this situation a parallel between Finny with his crippled leg and Philoctetes with his wounded leg, both of whom forgave and saved their betrayers.

PHINEAS AS HERO

Another level of meaning in the novel is the way it considers the predicament of a good man in a corrupt world. This timeless theme is seen in much of the world's great literature: the story of Joseph, Job, Christ, Hamlet, [Leo] Tolstoy's "Ivan the Fool," [Fyodor] Dostoevsky's *The Idiot*, and [Henrik] Ibsen's *An Enemy of the People*. Phineas of *A Separate Peace* is a brother to the central characters in these stories. He has the winning charm and nobility of spirit of these other heroes. Like them he is at variance with the corrupt world around him. During the idyllic summer session at Devon in 1942 while the rest of the world is engaged in an inhuman conflict, Finny is the leader of a small band of sixteen-year-olds who find a separate peace. When Gene remembers how perfect that summer was, he pictures Finny balanced joyfully on one foot on the front of a canoe going down the river, looking as though he were a god about to take off into the air, the embodiment of summer, youth, innocence, and goodness. After he is crippled and cannot hope to take part in World War II, Finny half playfully pretends and makes Gene pretend that the war is a fake, that it is all a charade created by corrupt, fat old men in order to prevent young people from taking away their power and luxuries. To Finny the rest of the world is a madhouse, a "Funny Farm."

The world usually will not tolerate a good man who sees through its corruption. It usually breaks and destroys the good man as it did Christ, Hamlet, and Prince Myshkin. It breaks Finny physically and almost breaks him spiritually, but after giving in temporarily to hate, he quickly regains his integrity. The world destroys his body, but not his spirit.

WAR AND PEACE

Probing the novel further for other levels of meaning, we find it is also a novel about war and peace. The war is the macrocosm of *A Separate Peace.* It is out there, remote from the mercifully, although temporarily, spared sixteen-year-olds in the blissful summer session at Devon. Finny and his small band of pals make up the microcosm. These boys at this time are too young for military training. The adult world looks on them with fond wistfulness, spoiling them a bit, allowing them to break a few rules, because the adults know that in a year or so these boys may be dying at the battlefronts. There seems to be an unspoken agreement to allow this age group to have a last fling at peace. Peace takes the form of frequent unscheduled swims in the river, missing meals to stay out and play longer, cutting classes, an illegal bike trip to the seashore for swimming and sleeping all night on the beach, making up an imaginative athletic game and playing it every day, and setting a new speed record in the school's swimming pool just for the fun of it and telling no one. After Finny's accident this special kind of peace disappears for a while, but then when Finny returns to school, peace comes back again, this time in the form of training Gene for the never-to-be-held 1944 Olympic Games and in the form of the glorious, wild Winter Carnival organized by Finny. The peace of this microcosm is epitomized by Finny dancing "his choreography of peace" on one leg (the other still in a cast) on the prize table.

The war, however, cannot be kept from encroaching occasionally on this island of peace. Food and luxury shortages increase. Large numbers of Devon boys are recruited to save the local apple crop and to shovel the Boston railroad yards out from under a paralyzing snowfall. But Gene and Finny do not feel the horror of the war until the first boy from Devon to enlist, Leper Lepellier, cracks up mentally during his basic training. The grim reality of Leper's failure makes Finny give up his playful fantasy that the war is a hoax. By contrasting the Devon idyl with the evil war of the outside world. Knowles lets us see that there is more sense in Finny's nonsense world of peace than in the real world of war.

GENE'S SEARCH FOR SELF-KNOWLEDGE

The deepest and most important level of meaning in *A Separate Peace* is the struggle for self-knowledge and maturity. To understand this meaning we must recognize that Gene, not Finny, is the central character of the book, just as the young sea captain, not Leggatt, is the central character of [Joseph] Conrad's *The Secret Sharer* and Marlow, not Kurtz,

is the central character of *The Heart of Darkness*. As in these
two Conrad works, which *A Separate Peace* resembles in
theme and purpose, the narrating central character (Gene)
identifies himself with another character (Finny) who occu-
pies most of his thoughts. Eventually in all three of these
novels the narrator finds himself through his identification
with the other person. Finny is such an admirable character
and he is talked about so much that there is a natural temptation to consider him the protagonist, but we should see
that the main struggle in the novel is Gene's.

Even when we first meet Finny, he knows who he is and
has a healthy way of facing life; he possesses unusual self-
confidence and wholeness for a boy so young. It is not sur-
prising that Gene and the other boys naturally look to him as
their leader. It is Gene who is lacking in wholeness. We see
this in his fear of jumping from the tree even though he is
quite capable of doing it successfully. We see it in his growing resentment of Finny's power over him. We see it in his
mistaken notion that Finny is trying to hurt his academic
record. We see it most of all when Gene shakes Finny from
the tree even after he knew that his suspicions of Finny were
unjust. This cruel act in the tree, however, marks the beginning of Gene's self-discovery. He courageously forces himself to see the savage darkness in his heart that caused him
to turn against Finny, and he manfully confesses to Finny.
Finny's rejection of the confession prevents Gene's immediate recovery. Gene must return to school in the fall spiritually maimed. His refusal to go out for sports is a sign of this.
When Finny calls Gene up long distance from his home and
offers his healing forgiveness, Gene's spirit begins to lose its
sickness: ". . . I lost part of myself to him then, and a soaring
sense of freedom revealed that this must have been my purpose from the first: to become a part of Phineas." In losing
himself to Finny he began to find himself.

Gene does not achieve self-knowledge and maturity, however, until after two more painful incidents in the novel,
Leper's breakdown and Finny's rebreaking of his leg. When
Gene visits Leper in his Vermont home after Leper's crack-
up and "escape" from the army, Leper with the unerring insight that his own illness gives him accuses Gene of always
being "a savage underneath" and cites his knocking Finny
out of the tree as evidence. Gene has to face this ugly truth
again as well as the possibility that he might lose his sanity

in the war just as Leper did. After the second breaking of Finny's leg Gene must relive his guilt, and Finny cannot reject the truth that was so clearly brought out at the mock investigation. In the hospital room both Gene and Finny face the truth about Gene, and about all mankind, the truth that there is a blind, ignorant, crazy evil in the heart of man.

After the agony of these experiences of self-realization, Gene can accept the death of Finny with manly sorrow but no weak tears, and he can enter the war without false heroism and without hating the enemy. He now understands the cause of war. He will not be driven out of his senses by the incomprehensibility of it as Leper was, and he will not childishly blame it on the older generation as Brinker does. Gene sees now "that wars were made instead by something ignorant in the human heart." He tells us that he has already killed his enemy. His enemy is his youthful innocence, personified by Finny; his enemy is his former ignorance of the darkness that lurks in his heart and in the hearts of all men.

OVERLAPPING THEMES

We have seen the complexity of *A Separate Peace* in six different levels of meaning, and further analysis would reveal others. The novel also possesses the necessary quality of unity. The unity can be observed in the overlapping of the ideas; the same characters and often the same major incidents illustrate each of the levels. But the unity is best seen in the way all the other meanings relate to and support the deepest meaning—the theme of self-knowledge. For example, a level of meaning discussed earlier, the relationship between Gene's fear and hate, is intimately related to Gene's struggle to know himself. He cannot know himself until he can identify and uproot the fear and hate that lie within his spirit. He is not mature until he recognizes that he, like his fellow men, is capable of blind fury and that it might overtake him again.

Another level of meaning previously examined, the understanding of sin and forgiveness, is also thoroughly intertwined with the primary theme of self-knowledge. Gene sins because he does not know himself or his *alter ego* Finny well enough. Finny's forgiveness of Gene cures Gene of his separation from Finny and from himself. The idea that Finny is a modern illustration of the good man in a corrupt world is closely tied in with the struggle for self-knowledge too. Although he is Finny's best friend, Gene represents, even better than the fat old men that Finny ridicules, the corruption of the world that destroys Finny. The essence of the world's corruption is that universal savagery of which a part is found in Gene's soul. Gene's discovery of this evil in himself while in the tree takes place at the same time as his betrayal of his friend and leads to the loss of Finny. The cost of self-discovery in a world as corrupt as ours is usually high. In this case the cost is the destruction of the one supremely good man Gene knows.

Finally, the novel's treatment of the conflict between war and peace further supports the theme of self-knowledge. Another part of Gene's gradual understanding of himself is his ridding himself of fear of the war. This vague fear of the war was part of his immaturity; it is another word for the enemy that he says he killed while still at school. In the conclusion of the novel Gene tells us how various other people tried to cope with the thought of war. Some tried to pretend that they were humble ants not worthy to be involved in such a gigantic menace. Some, like Mr. Ludsbury, tried, by asserting their superiority to the whole mess, to remain aloof from it. People like Quackenbush tried to fight it with practical schemes to avoid combat duty. Brinker and others like him took refuge in resentment against the older generation that supposedly caused the war. Others like Leper met the horror face to face and lost their minds. Only Finny knew how to regard the war or any other evil; his way was with confidence in himself, with no fear or hatred of anyone else, and with a sense that occasional bursts of animosity are part of everyone's human nature. Through his life and character he imparted this wisdom to Gene, and in this way Gene found himself and became a man.

A Study of Man's Bestiality

Peter Wolfe

According to Peter Wolfe, *A Separate Peace* is a study in mankind's inherent bestiality. Through Gene's hatred of Finny, Knowles poses the question: Is it possible for humans to bridle the primitive impulses that threaten to override reason and order? In a statement rich in underlying meaning, Gene seems to answer this question with an emphatic "no" when he insists that his vicious maiming of Finny was borne of "some ignorance inside me," an impulse that totally usurped reason and responsibility. Wolfe contributed this critical essay to *The University Review*, a publication of the University of Missouri.

John Knowles's concern with morality colors all his books. This preoccupation finds its most general expression in a question asked in *Double Vision* (1964), an informal travel journal: "Can man prevail against the bestiality he himself has struggled out of by a supreme effort?" Knowles's novels, instead of attacking the question head-on, go about it indirectly. They ask, first, whether a person can detach himself from his background—his society, his tradition, and the primitive energies that shaped his life.

The question is important because Knowles sees all of modern life shot through with malevolence. The sound the "frigid trees" make during a winter walk in *A Separate Peace* resembles "rifles being fired in the distance"; later, a character likens the rays of the sun to a volley of machine-gun fire. The book cries to be read in the context of original sin: its central event of a character falling from a tree: the snake-like rush of sibilants in "The Super Suicide Society of the Summer Session," an informal daredevil club whose founding leads to the novel's tragedy: an ocean wave that

Reprinted from Peter Wolfe, "The Impact of Knowles's *A Separate Peace*," *The University Review*, vol. 36, no. 3 (March 1970), pp. 189–98, by permission of the publisher. Notes and references in the original have been omitted in this reprint.

"hissed . . . toward the deep water" after upending a character: the "dead gray waves hissing mordantly along the beach" the next day.

This universal implication in guilt makes good a major premise of Knowles's fiction: that the condition of life is war. *A Separate Peace* describes the private battles of a prep school coterie boiling into the public fury of World War II. The individual and society are both at war again in Knowles's second novel, *Morning in Antibes* (1962), where the Algerian-French War invades the chic Riviera resort, Côte d'Azur. *Indian Summer* (1966) not only presents the World War II period and its aftermath as a single conflict-ridden epoch; it also describes civilian life as more dangerous than combat.

The Knowles hero, rather than tearing himself from his background, submerges himself in it. According to Knowles, man can only know himself through action; he learns about life by acting on it, not by thinking about it. The action is never collective, and it always involves treachery and physical risk.

THE CORE OF SELFHOOD

A full life to Knowles is one lived on the margins of disaster. Brinker Hadley in *A Separate Peace* and Neil Reardon in *Indian Summer* are both actionists, but since their lives are governed by prudence and not feeling they can never probe the quick of being. In order to touch the spontaneous, irrational core of selfhood, man must act unaided. At this point Knowles's ontology runs into the roadblock of original sin. Whereas the characters in his books who shrink from a bone-to-bone contact with life are labelled either escapists or cowards, the ones who lunge headlong into reality are usually crushed by the reality they discover. That all of Knowles's leading characters smash their closest friendship and also fall sick conveys the danger of a highly charged encounter with life.

This danger increases because of the way they go about the problem of self-being. Instead of struggling out of bestiality, to use Knowles's metaphor from *Double Vision,* they sink back into it. The Knowles hero moves forward by moving backward. *A Separate Peace* mentions "the deep tacit way in which feeling becomes stronger than thought," "that level of feeling, deeper than thought, which contains the truth," and "that deep layer of the mind where all is judged by the five senses and primitive expectation."

Prime being, then, is both sensory and prereflective, a tremor of uncensored energy. By obeying this dark urgency we can unleash a wildness that cuts down everything in its path. Gene Forrester insists that his shaking of his best friend, Phineas, out of a tree was prompted by "some ignorance inside me"; later he says that "wars were made . . . by something ignorant in the human heart." The first movers of our consciousnesses are "ignorant" in that they override reason and order. But unless we give them full rein we can never unroll our energies full force.

EMPHASIS ON AMERICAN CULTURE

A Separate Peace shapes the problem of man's inherent savagery to American culture. In contrast to the characters of D.H. Lawrence, those of Knowles do not discharge their deepest impulses sexually. Instead they retrace the familiar American fictional pattern of immersing themselves in the past. But where [F. Scott] Fitzgerald's Gatsby hankers after the glamor of first love and [Arthur] Miller's Willy Loman looks back to the days when salesmanship was adventurous, Knowles's Gene Forrester reaches back much further. He sounds the uncharted seas of our common humanity and in so doing both undoes the work of civilization and reawakens the wild meaninglessness of primitive man.

The novel's setting gives Gene's problem an American emphasis. In *Double Vision,* Knowles discusses the primitive barbarism underlying American life: "The American character is unintegrated, unresolved, a careful Protestant with a savage stirring in his insides, a germ of American wildness thickening in his throat." This elemental threat, Knowles continues, is all the more lethal for being hidden: "American life has an orderly, rather dull and sober surface, but with something berserk stirring in its depths."

Devon School in New Hampshire, "the most beautiful school in New England" and a haven of gentility, sportsmanship, and academic honors, has the same sort of deceptiveness. Its tame surface and schoolboy remoteness from World War II make it an unlikely setting for violence. As he does with the smiling, boyish soldiers who appear in the last chapter of the novel, Knowles uses a prep school setting to show that even innocence and beauty cannot escape the corrosive ooze of evil. (Devon's Field House is called suggestively "The Cage," indicating that bestiality is already in force at the school.) Contributing to the irony established by the disjuncture of cause and effect, or setting and event, is Knowles's quiet, understated style. That violence should leap so suddenly out of Knowles's offhand, conversational cadences sharpens the horror of the violence. (In *Double Vision*, Knowles praises E.M. Forster for his ability to stir his readers without raising his voice.)

GENE'S SELF-EXPLORATION

The first chapter of *A Separate Peace* shows Gene Forrester returning to Devon fifteen years after the key incident of his life—that of shaking his best friend Phineas out of a tree and shattering his leg. Mingling memory and fear, Gene is not only the archetypal criminal who returns to the scene of his crime or the American fictional hero who retreats into a private past. His return to Devon is purposive, even compulsive. His neglecting to mention his job, his family, or his home suggests that he has none of these things, even though he is past the age of thirty. He relives his act of treachery and the events surrounding it in the hope of recovering the separate peace of the summer of 1942.

Gene interests us chiefly because of his moral ambiguity: whereas he accepts his malevolence, he also resists indulging it at the expense of others. Fear of unleashing his inherent wickedness explains his inertia since Devon's 1942–43 academic year. It also explains his psychological bloc. His first-person narration is laced with self-abuse, special pleading, flawed logic, and evasiveness. As has been suggested, self-exploration is dangerous work, and Gene cannot be blamed if he sometimes cracks under the strain. Out of joint with both himself and his time, he subjects to reason an area of being which is neither rational nor reducible to rational formulas. Although the sum will not add, he has no choice but to try to add the sum if he wants to re-enter the human community.

THE FOREST

Like the novel's memoir technique, Gene Forrester's name certifies that *A Separate Peace* is his book. Of the forest, Gene is a primitive, bloodthirsty woodlander; his occasional self-disclosures spell out the urgency of his death-pull: "I was used to finding something deadly in things that attracted me; there was always something deadly lurking in anything I wanted, anything I loved. And if it wasn't there . . . I put it there myself."

The forest has negative associations throughout the book.

At one point Gene is accused of undermining his health by "smoking like a forest fire." Elsewhere the forest is equated with the raw icy wilderness stretching from the northern edge of Devon School to "the far unorganized tips of Canada." As it is in Emily Dickinson, summer for Knowles is the time of flowing beauty and intensity of being. The Sommers family are the most vital characters in *Indian Summer*, and the gipsy spree of Gene and Phineas takes place during summer term.

Devon represents the last outpost of civilization to Gene. It wards off the primitive madness encroaching from the great northern forests, and it shields its students from the organized madness of World War II. Devon's 1942 summer term, the first in its history, is giving Gene and Phineas their last reprieve from a war-racked world. At sixteen, the boys and their classmates are the oldest students at Devon excused from taking both military subjects and preinduction physical exams.

In contrast to this freedom, winter brings loss, unreason, and hardness of heart. Nor is the heartless irrationality equated with Gene's forest background uncommon. His first name universalizes his glacial cruelty. While Phineas is a sport (who happens to excel in sports), Gene is generic, his barbarism deriving from his North American forebears. And the fact that he is a southerner shows how deeply this northern madness has bitten into American life.

THE TREE

The first object of Gene's return visit to Devon is the tree he ousted Phineas from fifteen years before. James Ellis places the tree in a Christian context by calling it "the Biblical tree of knowledge." His interpretation is amply justified by parallels between the novel and orthodox Christianity: everything in the boys' lives changes for the worst after the tree incident, the tree and Christ's crucifix are both wood, the slab of light under the door that announces Phineas's return to Devon is yellow, the color of Judas and betrayal, and Gene chins himself thirty times the next day in the school's gymnasium.

Yet Christian myth fails to exhaust the tree's meaning. Its rootedness in the earth, its riverbank location, and its overarching branches suggest organic life. Lacking a single meaning, the tree stands for reality itself. Knowles develops this powerful inclusiveness by projecting the tree to several levels of being. For the tree not only exists forcibly at more than one dimension; it also brings together different aspects of reality. Over the spectrum of Gene's life, it is by turns an occasion for danger, friendship, betrayal and regret. Remembered as "a huge lone spike dominating the riverbank, forbidding as an artillery piece," the tree is so much "smaller" and "shrunken by age" fifteen years later that Gene has trouble recognizing it.

Nonetheless, as something more than a physical datum, it marks the turning point of Gene's life and colors the rest of his narrative. The furniture in the home of one of his teachers "shot out menacing twigs," and the tree combines metaphorically with both the War and the aboriginal northern frost to create a strong impression of lostness. The tree's combining power, in fact, is as great as its power to halt or cut short. For while it marks the end of the gipsy summer of 1942, it also yokes Gene's past and present lives.

The victim of the tree incident, Phineas, is best summarized by a phrase Knowles uses in *Double Vision* to describe modern Greeks—"a full life lived naturally." Nor is the classical parallel askew. Phineas's name resembles phonetically that of Phidias, who helped set the standard of all-around excellence that marked the golden age of Pericles. (The nickname, "Finny," suggests in another key a throwback to a morality earlier than our Christian-western ethical system.) Although "an extraordinary athlete . . . the best athlete in the school," Finny stands under five feet nine and weighs only a hundred and fifty pounds. His athletic prowess stems not from brawn but from his superb co-ordination and vitality.

Interestingly, the trophies he wins are for gentlemanly conduct. Finny's mastery goes beyond sports. His great gift is the ability to respond clearly and fully: his "unthinking unity of movement" and his favorite expressions "naturally" and "perfectly okay," express the harmony and interrelatedness of his life. Finny can afford casualness because he gives himself wholly to his undertakings. There is no room for self-consciousness in this dynamic life-mode. There is no room either for formalized rules. Finny's commitment to life overrides the requirements of reason and law, but not out of innate lawlessness. His responses strike so deeply that, while they sometimes make nonsense of conventional morality, they create their own scale of values.

MAN: A HATING ANIMAL

Finny's organicism also sets the style and tempo of the free, unclassifiable summer of 1942. It must be noted that the separate peace Finny and Gene carve out is no idyllic escape from reality. By founding the Super Suicide Society of the Summer Session, membership in which requires a dangerous leap into the Devon River, the boys admit both danger and death into their golden gipsy days. Accordingly, the game of Blitzball, which Finny invents the same summer, includes the bellicosity and treachery that perhaps count as humanity's worst features: "Since we're all enemies, we can and will turn on each other all the time." Nevertheless, the boys rejoice in Blitzball and, while they sustain a fierce level of competition, they manage to avoid injuries.

For opponents do not inflict pain in the world of *A Separate Peace;* the worst menaces dwell not in rivalry but in friendship. Gene and Phineas become best friends, but Gene cannot live with Finny's goodness. Finny's helping Gene overcome fear and his opening his friend to bracing new adventures rouses Gene's worst traits. Man is a hating rather than a loving animal. Franziska Lynne Greiling summarizes deftly the stages leading to Gene's savaging of Finny:

> At the beginning, Gene thought of himself as Phineas' equal, first in excellence, then in enmity. Discovering Phineas incapable of hatred, Gene has to face his own moral ugliness and then strikes down Phineas for inadvertently revealing it to him.

The summary bears close scrutiny. What finally unlooses Gene's venom is Finny's magnanimity. Although Gene's treachery in Chapter Four strikes explosively, incidents in earlier chapters justify it dramatically. Finny's saving Gene at the end of Chapter Two when he nearly falls out of the tree during a mission of the Super Suicide Society compounds his felony. Gene turns the act of loyalty and sacrifice into an occasion for resentment. Instead of being grateful to Finny for saving his life, he blames his friend for tempting him to jump from the tree in the first place.

BESTIALITY UNLEASHED

Chapter Three puts Finny beyond such commonplace resentment. Here he breaks the school's swimming record for the hundred-yard free style but insists that his feat be kept a secret. Chapter Four shows Gene incontestably that Finny has both outclassed and outmanned him. Whereas Gene bases all his human ties on rivalry, he must bolt down the knowledge that Finny is free of envy. This generosity upsets Gene's entire life-mode: "Now I knew that there never was and never could have been any rivalry between us. I was not of the same quality as he."

Of all modern psychoanalytical theories, perhaps Adler's doctrine of masculine protest best explains Gene's malignancy. But even Adler falls short; Gene's cruelty is unconscious and it brings him no prizes. Nothing so simple as worldly success is at stake in the tree incident. For Gene is one of Devon's best students, and he knows that his gifts, although less spectacular than Finny's, are more durable.

Besides having time in his favor, Gene is already Finny's equal: "I was more and more certainly becoming the best student in the school; Phineas was without question the best athlete, so in that way we were even. But while he was a very poor student, I was a pretty good athlete, and when everything was thrown into the scales they would in the end tilt definitely toward me."

By shaking his friend out of the tree, Gene obeys an urge deeper than reason or wounded vanity. But his act of aboriginal madness is empty. The things that happen to him after his treachery demonstrates the pointless waste of violence.

But they do not draw the sting of his violent tendencies. Gene's first reaction to Finny's shattered leg is complex. Since Finny's vitality diminishes Gene, he is glad to be rid of his friend. Finny's confinement in the Infirmary lets Gene become Finny. He calls Finny "noble" and in the next paragraph, after putting on his friend's clothes, says that he feels "like some nobleman." Even the relaxed, supple style in which he writes his memoir fits with his desire to merge with his male ideal.

Ironically, Finny is just as eager as Gene to switch identities. Rather than accusing him of treachery or languishing in self-pity, he tries to recover some of his lost splendor through his friend. Knowles says at one point in the book that a broken bone, once healed, is strongest in the place where the break occurred. The statement applies to Finny's recuperative powers. His athletic career ended, Finny acquires new skills and learns to exist on a new plane while preserving his high standard of personal loyalty.

Everything and nothing have changed. Buoyed up by his heroic ethic, he returns to Devon midway through the winter term and begins training Gene for the 1944 Olympic Games. His training a groundling athlete for a match that will never be held points up the strength of his moral vision. Finny denies the reality of World War II because he knows instinctively that man can only fulfill himself when the ordinary civilized processes of life are reasonably secure.

The two boys institute a routine based on their best gifts: while Finny coaches Gene on the cinderpath and in the gym, Gene helps Finny with his studies. The routine is kinetic. Finny's organizing of the Devon Winter Carnival, like the Blitzball and the Super Suicide Society of the previous summer, represents an acceptance of reality. But the Carnival reflects an even braver commitment to imperfection than the summer romps. It takes no special gifts to make merry in the summer. By celebrating winter, though, Phineas opts for life's harshness as well as its joys; and by choosing the northern reaches of the school as a site for the carnival, he certifies fun and friendship alongside the icy savagery clawing down from the unpeopled North.

GENE'S DETACHMENT

Gene ends this regimen because he cannot forgive Phineas for submitting to his brutality. He determines to make his cruelty a counterforce to Phineas's loyalty and courage. After Phineas breaks his leg falling on the slick marble steps of the First Academy Building, Gene follows him to the Infirmary. But instead of showing compassion for his stricken friend, his thoughts turn inward. Astonishingly, his attitude is one of cool self-acceptance. "I couldn't escape a confusing sense of living through all of this before—Phineas in the Infirmary, and myself responsible. I seemed to be less shocked by it now than I had been the first time last August."

Gene's detachment imparts the final horror to his actions. Yet Phineas can take his worst thrusts. Although he can no longer control his muscular reactions, his mind stays whole. His body breaks before his spirit; he accepts Gene's treachery, and when he dies he has transcended it. Nobody in the book can come near enough to him to kill him. He dies as he had lived—untouched by human baseness. While his broken leg is being set, some of the bone-marrow escapes into his bloodstream and lodges in his heart. In that bone-marrow produces the body's life-giving red corpuscles, Phineas dies from an overplus and a richness of animal vigor.

THE LEPER-FINNY MOTIF

Gene's barbarism finds another outlet in Elwin "Leper" Lepellier. Although Leper is not so well perceived as Finny, he serves structurally as Finny's foil. Whereas Finny attracts people, Leper is an outsider; and Leper matches Finny's physical breakdown by cracking psychologically. A solitary at school, he is crushed by the tighter discipline and organization practiced by the Army. But the organized madness of the Army, while wrecking his sanity, sharpens his insight. He tells Gene, "You always were a savage underneath," and later in the book he describes the tree episode with a poetic accuracy that lays bare the core of Gene's treachery.

Yet none of Leper's hearers can understand him. Finny, on the other hand, communicates by bodily movements and is always perfectly understood. Leper's oppositeness to Finny reveals two important things about Gene's savagery: its all-inclusive sweep and its static nature. Although Finny and Leper both grow, Gene is hunkered in his wickedness. In the same way that primitive societies are the least free, he can neither explain nor change himself once he gives in to his primitive drives. Not only does he rake his two best friends; he justifies his butchery: "a mind was clouded and a leg was broken—maybe these should be thought of as minor and inevitable mishaps in the accelerating rush. The air around us was filled with much worse things."

The Leper-Finny doubling motif is but one example of Knowles's fondness for sharp contrast as a structural principle. The author also plays the carefree summer of 1942 against the winter term that follows. He manages his contrast by means of the various associations created by the intervening season, fall.

Finny's fall from the tree by the river, in ending the boys' summer, draws the warmth and light from Devon. Gene notices a chill in the air even before the start of the new term in September: "I knew now it was fall all right." In a telephone call the same day, Phineas tells Gene that he was "completely over the falls" the last time the two boys visited together. Even the elements seem convulsed, as the fight between *Gene Forrester* and *Cliff* Quacken*bush* by the *river* suggests. The fight also underscores the emptiness of Gene's ravage upon Finny. As soon as Devon's winter term starts without Finny, Gene's status declines. The assistant crew manager's job Gene takes carries no prestige, and his fight with Cliff Quackenbush, one of Devon's most unpopular students, is just as pointless.

The daily character of life at Devon also expresses the darkening shift from summer to winter. The change in mood is

observable the first day of winter term: "We had been an idiosyncratic, leaderless band in the summer. . . . Now the official class leaders and politicians could be seen taking
charge." Gene's murder of the "simple, unregulated friendliness" marking the summer term validates the need for restricting man's freedom. Like that of [Nathaniel] Hawthorne,
Knowles's attitude toward the law is complex. If civilization
is to survive, then man's intrinsic savagery must be bridled.
Yet any formal legal system will prove unreliable. The members of the older generation described in the book cannot
claim any natural or acquired superiority over their sons.
They stand to blame for the War and also for the congres-
sional investigating committees the novel attacks indirectly.

BRINKER THE LAWGIVER

Rules and restrictions turn out to be just as poor a standard
of civilized conduct as feelings. Knowles introduces the
character of Brinker Hadley—a classmate of Finny, Leper,
and Gene—to point up the murderous cruelty of the law. Significantly, Brinker does not enter the book until the 1942–43
winter term. He makes the distressing point that man tends
to use the law not as a check to man's aggressiveness, but as
an outlet. Legalistic, rule-bound, and calculating, Brinker
only invokes the law in order to frustrate or to punish.
Knowles mentions "his Winter Session efficiency" and later
calls him "Brinker the Lawgiver" and "Justice incarnate."

But he also reminds us that although Justice balances the
scales of human conduct, she is also blindfolded. Brinker's
blind spot is the life of feeling, his fact-ridden life having
ruled out compassion. Brinker, who has a large posterior, or
butt, presides from the Butt Room, a cellar which is both the
dreariest and the lowest site on the Devon campus. Because
Gene could not rise to the example set by Phineas, he must
pass muster with Brinker's Butt-Room morality. The tree incident not only drives the boys indoors but also downward—
both physically and morally:

> The Butt Room was something like a dungeon. . . . On the
> playing fields we looked like innocent extroverts; and in the
> Butt Room we looked, very strongly, like criminals. The
> school's policy, in order to discourage smoking, was to make
> these rooms as depressing as possible.

The structure of *A Separate Peace* includes the same tensions, stresses, and balances. Chapter Seven, the middle chap-

ter of the novel, is dominated by snow, a common symbol for death. Suitably, the big snowfall of Chapter Seven, like the tree incident of Chapter Four, occurs out of season. Chapter Seven also introduces Brinker Hadley and restores Phineas to Devon. As the chapter advances, the thickening snows envelop Gene; by the end of the chapter, they obstruct all of life.

On the day of Phineas's return, two hundred Devon students volunteer to shovel the snow from the tracks of a local railroad yard. The heavy work, the trainful of soldiers that passes by, and the sickly, quarrelsome foreman of the snow removal combine to make this "misbegotten day" an epitome of death. Finny's coming back to school in November, finally, changes Gene's mind about enlisting. With Finny as a roommate, Gene does not need the War as an outlet for his aggressiveness.

Gene's visit to Finny's home in Boston in Chapter Five and his visit to Leper's in Chapter Ten contain enough striking similarities and differences to stand as mutually explanatory. In Chapter Ten Leper, painfully disoriented after his abortive tour of military service, accuses Gene of having deliberately knocked Phineas out of the tree the previous summer. Gene hotly denies the charge and goes on to abuse and then desert Leper during his crisis: "I was the closest person in the world to him now." Chapter Five, curiously, shows Gene confessing the same treachery and Finny defending him to himself.

The two chapters mirror each other nearly perfectly: Gene reverses field completely, and Finny's self-command balances Leper's mental collapse. But Gene's shift in roles from self-accuser to self-defender is flawed. He shows Leper none of the kindness extended by Finny in Chapter Five, even though his moral situation in Chapter Ten is less difficult than Finny's was.

Gene's failure is one of moral escapism. When Leper reveals himself as a misfit in a world where nothing fits with anything else, Gene flees. Leper's description of the ugliness and disjointedness underlying life strikes Gene so hard that he must deny it in order to keep peace with himself: "I didn't want to hear any more of it. Not now or ever. I didn't care because it had nothing to do with me."

Another pair of incidents whose variations clarify theme take place in Chapter Three and Chapter Eleven—the third chapter from the end of the novel. The element of Chapter Three is water: Finny breaks Devon's swimming record for the hundred-yard free style, and then swims for an hour in the ocean. By Chapter Eleven the water has frozen.

INTENTIONAL DISCORD

After walking out of a mock-serious investigation of the tree incident, Finny falls a second time and breaks his leg on the "unusually hard" white marble steps of the First Academy Building. His flowing energy has been immobilized both by Leper's mental breakdown and the loveless efficiency of the investigation. A fact does not count for Finny until he experiences it personally; his head-on encounters with pain and heartlessness kill his belief in universal harmony, and he can no longer deny the ubiquity of war. His separate peace ended, he merges in the last paragraph of Chapter Eleven with the icy discord that gores all of life:

> The excellent exterior acoustics recorded his rushing steps and the quick rapping of his cane. . . . Then these separate sounds collide into the general tumult of his body falling clumsily down the white marble stairs.

The technique of the last chapter tallies well with both the events and the morality it describes. Knowles violates the unity of time by leaping ahead several months to June 1943; he also breaks a basic rule of fictional art by introducing an important character in his last chapter. These discordancies are intentional: a novel about disjointedness should have its components out of joint with each other. Accordingly, *A Separate Peace* extends a chapter after Phineas's death and funeral.

But instead of joining its dramatic and thematic climaxes, the last chapter has a scattering effect. Gene's class at Devon has just been graduated, and the boys are shipping out to various branches of the military. The new character, Brinker Hadley's father, is a World War I veteran whose lofty code of patriotism and service means little to the younger generation.

Mr. Hadley cannot, however, be dismissed as a stale anachronism. His argument implies that he knows something the boys have not yet learned. Combat duty is important to him, not as an immediate goal but as a topic to reminisce about in future years. Could Mr. Hadley be suggesting that maturity contains few pleasures and that only a heroic youth can make up for this emptiness? That the boys overlook this implication means little. The chapter is full of communication failures, including the generation rift Mr. Hadley introduces by visiting Devon.

Another new presence at Devon is the U. S. Army. Devon has donated part of its grounds to a Parachute Riggers' school.

Appropriately, the sector of the campus used by the soldiers is the Northern Common. But Knowles pulls a stunning reversal by overturning this fine narrative stroke. For although the Army as the collective embodiment of man's aggressiveness invades Devon from the icy North, man's aggressiveness has already established a stronghold at Devon. Likewise, the convoy of jeeps driving through campus stirs no warlike fervor. The boyish troops are "not very bellicose-looking," and the jeeps do not contain weapons but sewing machines.

The logic of the novel makes eminent sense of this unlikely freight: the sewing machines, which will service parachutes, allude to the novel's central metaphor of falling, and the young soldiers will lunge headlong into violence in the same way as Devon's Class of 1943. By the end of the book, the malevolence uncoiling from man's fallen nature has engulfed all.

A FALSE PEACE

Except, strangely, for Gene. His savagery already spent, he has no aggressiveness left for the Navy. Although his country is at war, he is at peace. Yet the armistice is false. A man so askew with his environment enjoys no peace. Gene's lack of purpose not only divides him from his country; it separates him from himself. Divided and subdivided, he is fighting a war just as dangerous as his country's. He has not killed his enemy, as he insists.

His return to Devon in his early thirties and his memoir of Devon's 1942–43 academic year prove that his private struggle has outlasted the public holocaust of World War II. Just as the anvil can break the hammer, the tree incident hurts Gene more than it does Finny. The novel turns on the irony that the separate peace mentioned in its title excludes its most vivid presence—its narrator. Gene's fall 1957 visit to Devon fixes the limits of his fallen life. His self-inventory is either a preparation for life or a statement of withdrawal. But the question of whether he can convert his apartness into a new start goes beyond the boundaries of the novel.

Fear as Impetus

Jay L. Halio

Jay L. Halio praises *A Separate Peace* for its taut
style and careful handling of theme, which he
identifies as the fear that drives destructive hatred.
Indeed, Gene's vicious act against Finny is borne of
fear. This fear colors not only the carefree adolescent
life of a New England prep school but also the world
at large; the same destructive force that unleashes
Gene's worst traits is the impulse that causes the
war against which the novel is set. Halio contributed
the following critical essay to *Studies in Short
Fiction.*

At a time when best-sellerdom has fostered many overwrit-
ten, overpublicized, and often overpraised novels like James
Jones's *From Here to Eternity*, William Styron's *Set This House
on Fire*, and most recently Philip Roth's *Letting Go*, the problem of how to say much and say it well—in the compass of
about two hundred normal-sized pages—has become serious.
It has become a challenge to the writer who wishes to go beyond the limitations of the short story in order to develop the
full complexities of his theme without at the same time dissi-
pating his art and his energies in much padded or repetitive
verbiage. Among young writers it is therefore heartening to
see a few like John Knowles who, taking his cue from *The Sun
Also Rises* rather than from *For Whom the Bell Tolls*, has
brought back to recent fiction some of the clear craftsman-
ship and careful handling of form that characterizes our earlier and best fiction in this century.

EXPLORATION OF THE SELF

It is also heartening to see that among the same writers
many have shown an unremitting preoccupation with the
exploration of the self—a preoccupation, too, of earlier writers, both at home and abroad, but now somewhat relieved of

Abridged from Jay L. Halio, "John Knowles's Short Novels," *Studies in Short Fiction*,
vol. 1, no. 2 (Winter 1964), pp. 107–12. Copyright 1964 by Newberry College. Reprinted
with permission.

impinging social concerns, though not (which would be a poorer thing) totally divorced from them. The prevailing attitude seems to be that before man can be redeemed back into social life, he must first come to terms with himself, he must first—as has been said so often of American writers—discover who and what he is. That we must look inward and learn to face honestly what we see there and then move onwards or anyway outwards is necessary if in the long run we are to salvage any part of our humanity—if, indeed, humanity is in the future to have any meaning or value. This is the enterprise carried forward in contemporary literature by such novelists as Angus Wilson in England and Saul Bellow at home; and alongside their novels John Knowles has now placed [a] brilliant piece of fiction, *A Separate Peace.* . . . In his first novel, Knowles achieves a remarkable success in writing about adolescent life at a large boy's school without falling into any of the smart-wise idiom made fashionable by *The Catcher in the Rye* and ludicrously overworked by its many imitators.

A Separate Peace is the story of a small group of boys growing up at an old New England prep school called Devon during the early years of World War II. The principal characters are the narrator, Gene Forrester, and his roommate, Phineas, or "Finny," who has no surname. As yet but remotely aware of the war in Europe or the Pacific, the boys give themselves up during Devon's first summer session to sports and breaking school rules under the instigations of the indefatigable Finny. It is the last brief experience of carefree life they will know, for most of them will graduate the following June. But within this experience, another kind of war subtly emerges, a struggle between Gene, who is a good student and an able competitor in sports, and Finny, who is the school's champion athlete but poor at studying. Believing Finny's instigations aim at ruining his chances to become valedictorian of their class—and so upset the delicate balance of their respective achievements—Gene awakens to a mistaken sense of deadly enmity between them. (Anyone who has attended such schools will immediately recognize this conflict between intellectual and athletic glory.) Impulsively, Gene causes his roommate to fall from a tree during one of their more spectacular games, and cripples him. This is the central episode of the novel, and the fear which lies behind such destructive hatred is its major theme.

GENE'S FEAR

How Gene eventually loses this fear, and so is able to enter that other war without hatred, without the need to kill, is the business of the succeeding episodes. Confession by Gene of deliberate viciousness is alone insufficient release; indeed, far from bringing release, it causes deeper injury to Finny and to himself because of its basic half-truth. Freedom comes only after an honest confrontation of both his own nature and that extension of it represented by Finny, whose loss at the end of the novel he must somehow accept and endure. For if, as the book shows, Finny is unfit for war, and hence unfit for a world engaged in a chronic condition of war, it is because of his fundamental innocence or idealism—his regard for the world not as it is, but as it should be—that renders him unfit.

CONTROLLED ELOQUENCE

As many critics have noted, Knowles's narrative is understated and economical, yet stirring and evocative. The following excerpt from A Separate Peace *is clear testament to Knowles's quiet eloquence.*

A little fog hung over the river so that as I neared it I felt myself becoming isolated from everything except the river and the few trees beside it. The wind was blowing more steadily here, and I was beginning to feel cold. I never wore a hat, and had forgotten gloves. There were several trees bleakly reaching into the fog. Any one of them might have been the one I was looking for. Unbelievable that there were other trees which looked like it here. It had loomed in my memory as a huge lone spike dominating the riverbank, forbidding as an artillery piece, high as the beanstalk. Yet here was a scattered grove of trees, none of them of any particular grandeur.

Moving through the soaked, coarse grass I began to examine each one closely, and finally identified the tree I was looking for by means of certain small scars rising along its trunk, and by a limb extending over the river, and another thinner limb growing near it. This was the tree, and it seemed to me standing there to resemble those men, the giants of your childhood, whom you encounter years later and find that they are not merely smaller in relation to your growth, but that they are absolutely smaller, shrunken by age. In this double demotion the old giants have become pigmies while you were looking the other way.

John Knowles, *A Separate Peace.* New York: Bantam Books, 1960.

Under Finny's influence, most of the summer of 1942 was, for Gene, just such a world; and it is briefly restored during the following winter when, after convalescing, Phineas returns to Devon. But the existence of this world, and the separate peace this world provides, is doomed. In Finny's fall from the tree Gene has violated, or rather surrendered, his innocence, and he learns that any attempt to regain it, to "become part of Phineas," is at best a transient experience, at worst a gesture of despair. Nor will either of the twin expedients, escape or evasion, serve him. Escape, as it presents itself to Gene after Finny's second fall, the final crisis in the novel, is rejected as "not so much criminal as meaningless, a lapse into nothing, an escape into nowhere." And evasion—any recourse into the various dodges of sentimentality, such as aggressive arrogance, insensitive factionalism, or self-protective vagueness, as variously portrayed by other boys at Devon—such evasion, Gene comes to realize, is only a mask behind which one does not so much seek reality, as hide from it, for it is a mask to cover fear. "Only Phineas never was afraid, only Phineas never hated anyone," the book concludes. The essential harmony of his nature could not allow such emotions, and his "choreography of peace" in a world he alone could create and sustain, as for example during Devon's first, only, and illegal "Winter Carnival," is not the dance of this world. His death, coming as it does on the eve of graduation, is, then, for Gene a kind of necessary sacrifice before he can take the next step. And his forgiveness is Gene's way of forgiving himself for what he at last recognizes is "something ignorant in the human heart," the impersonal, blind impulse that caused Finny's fall and that causes war. It is an acceptance, too, the acceptance of a reality which includes ignorance and prepares for humility, without which the next step remains frozen in mid-air.

The Theme of Freedom

Franziska Lynne Greiling

Franziska Lynne Greiling compares elements of *A Separate Peace* to Greek ideas, specifically the Greek theme of freedom and its effects on the novel's protagonists. Finny's love of freedom and respect for the individual over rigid societal rules, for example, reflects the Greek ideal of harmony. Finny's downfall is his innocence, his inability to assimilate Gene's sins and his own losses. Unlike Finny, however, Gene gains an understanding of himself. Consequently, Gene redeems his guilt and frees himself of envy and despair. Greiling was on the faculty of the English Department at Highland Park High School in Highland Park, Michigan.

Phineas, charming hypnotic Phineas who "didn't know yet that he was unique," couldn't maintain the innocent freedom of the summer celebrated in *A Separate Peace.* The destruction begins with Gene's outburst of anger and is completed by rule-bound, insensitive Brinker. In the May 1964 *English Journal*, James Ellis detailed Knowles' use of Christian themes in "*A Separate Peace*, The Fall from Innocence." The topic of this article will be not innocence but freedom, the Greek theme of *A Separate Peace.*

Knowles makes a number of obvious references to the Greeks: the burning of *The Iliad* to begin the games at the Winter Carnival, the importance of athletics and the Olympics to Phineas, the Grecian sun "sharp and hard" on the frozen New Hampshire landscape when Gene goes to learn about Leper, and in such context, the repeated use of the words "freedom," "harmony," and "unity." All these are fragments from the Greek themes in the book. Knowles is concerned with the implications of certain Greek ideas: the necessity and effects of freedom, and its corollary ideal of arete: the individual's fulfillment of his own excellences—

From Franziska Lynne Greiling, "The Theme of Freedom in *A Separate Peace*," *English Journal*, vol. 56, no. 9 (December 1967), pp. 1269–72. Copyright 1967 by the National Council of Teachers of English. Reprinted with permission. References in the original have been omitted in this reprint.

moral, physical, intellectual, and political. In the first half, Phineas reflects these concerns. Phineas has a love of excellence and fulfills his ability in the discipline of athletics. When Finny understands that Gene must study to satisfy his ability as a scholar, he says:

> We kid around a lot and everything, but you have to be serious sometime, about something. If you're really good at something, I mean if there's nobody or hardly anybody, who's as good as you are, then you've got to be serious about that. Don't mess around, for God's sake.

Phineas represents Greek ideas more than Christian in another way. One of the basic contrasts between the two philosophies is that the Christians trust in God while the Greeks believed in man. In John 14:6, Jesus says: "I am the way, the truth, and the life; no man cometh unto the father but by me." Hippocrates, who took medicine from the care of the gods to scientific study by man, said: "Life is short, art is long, the occasion instant, experiment perilous, decision difficult." The contrast emphasizes the Greek awareness of the limitations and the greatness of man. Finny represents Greek more than Christian ideas when he respects the individual, not inviolable rules. He trusts too much, however. Finny lacks Hippocrates' mature awareness that while there is much to respect in man, he is vulnerable to time and ignorance.

FINNY'S IDEALISM

Phineas' respect for others is one of the reasons he lives successfully outside the rules. Finny loves freedom because in it, he can create "a flow of simple, unregulated friendliness . . . and such flows were one of Finny's reasons for living." Finny's charm and his delight in giving pleasure to others allow him to lead other people to break the rules. Phineas "considered authority the necessary evil against which happiness was achieved by reaction." Finny himself does not need rules to keep him good; he has an inner harmony, a humanity which allows him to respond with affection and generosity to even the rule-givers who must punish him. Phineas assumes that others would be his equals if only they would ignore the rules. He cannot understand that rules protect individuals from their own and others' weaknesses. He does not comprehend fear, envy, rage at one's own moral ugliness, nor the desire for revenge; so he uneasily ignores these in the individual and in their public

manifestation—the war. In Phineas is an idealism and innocence which protect him from seeing life as it is, but these
also cause him to try to create around him his ideal world.
In the novel, the best and last example of this special ability
is Finny's Winter Carnival. Here, Finny's denial of war, of
evil really, is most successful, and the festival has risen to
anarchy and inspiration.

> The hard cider began to take charge of us. Or I wonder now
> whether it wasn't cider but our own exuberance which in-
> toxicated us, sent restraint flying, causing Brinker to throw a
> football block on the statue of the Headmaster, giving me, as
> I put on the skiis and slid down the small slope and off the
> miniature ski jump a sensation of soaring flight, of hurtling
> high and far through space; inspiring Phineas, during one of
> Chet's Spanish inventions, to climb onto the Prize Table and
> with only one leg to create a droll dance among the prizes,
> springing and spinning from one bare space to another,
> cleanly missing Hazel Brewster's hair, never marring by a
> misstep the pictures of Betty Grable. Under the influence not
> I know of the hardest cider but of his own inner joy at life for
> a moment as it should be, as it was meant to be in his nature,
> Phineas recaptured that magic gift for existing primarily in
> space, one foot conceding briefly to gravity its rights before
> spinning him off again into the air. It was his wildest demon-
> stration of himself, of himself in the kind of world he loved; it
> was his choreography of peace.

Appropriate to his defensive innocence, Phineas begins the
games by burning *The Iliad.* And here is his flaw, Phineas
does not fulfill one of the most prized Greek virtues—intellectual excellence. To Phineas, "freedom" is not the opportunity to "Know thyself."

Perhaps his imperfection makes him all the more Greek.
Yet Phineas does partake of the combination of moral and
physical beauty that Plato described in *The Republic.*

> And the absence of grace, rhythm, harmony is nearly allied to
> baseness of thought and expression and baseness of charac-
> ter: whereas their presence goes with that moral excellence
> and self-mastery of which they are the embodiment.

Phineas' physical beauty and personal harmony remind one
of two fifth-century Greek sculptures: Myron's Discobolus
and Polyclitus' Doryphorus. The body of the Discus Thrower
is slender and competent, the face is serene, revealing an inner calm. The agony of violent effort is absent in this disciplined athlete. The Doryphorus depicts an athlete after performance who, like the Discus Thrower, is unmarked by
effort. He walks with a unified, flowing movement, and his

face reveals a quiet, inner fulfillment. Both statues reflect a Greek idealism and both express a Greek poise: pride without egotism and self-confidence without complacency. Phineas' poise, like that of fifth-century Greece, is vulnerable. As the Greeks feared, the weakness was in man's inadequate knowledge of himself and his world. During the decline of Greece, the resulting loss of confidence is evident in sculpture. In the Laocoon, heavily muscled figures struggle against inevitable defeat. These subjects have no harmonious relationship with the cosmos. In *A Separate Peace*, Gene destroys Phineas' unity by committing an act which Phineas cannot assimilate into his view of life.

> All others at some point found something in themselves pitted violently against something in the world around them. With those of my year this point often came when they grasped the fact of the war. When they began to feel that there was this overwhelmingly hostile thing in the world with them, then the simplicity and unity of their characters broke and they were not the same again.

> Phineas alone had escaped this. He possessed an extra vigor, a heightened confidence in himself, a serene capacity for affection which saved him. Nothing as he was growing up at home, nothing at Devon, nothing even about the war had broken his harmonious and natural unity. So at last I had.

Like the figures of the Laocoon, Phineas is unable to survive when he is betrayed. Gene's is the agonized struggle.

GENE'S SINS

At the beginning, Gene thought of himself as Phineas' equal, first in excellence, then in enmity. Discovering Phineas incapable of hatred, Gene has to face his own moral ugliness and then strikes down Phineas for inadvertently revealing it to him. Rules are unnecessary and restricting for Phineas, but Gene has need of the rules, for he lacks the humanity to make the generous response to others. Gene fails the high demands of freedom, accepts himself as evil, and retreats to the rules.

> It was forced on me as I sat chilled through the chapel service, that this probably vindicated the rules of Devon after all, wintry Devon. If you broke the rules, then they broke you.

In despair, Gene considers committing himself to the evil in his nature. Knowles implies that such action would be a form of death for Gene by alluding to the myth of the Greek fates.

To enlist. To slam the door impulsively on the past, to shed everything down to my last bit of clothing, to break the pattern of my life—that complex design I had been weaving since birth with all its dark threads, its unexplainable symbols set against a conventional background of domestic white and schoolboy blue, all those tangled strands which required the dexterity of a virtuoso to keep flowing—I yearned to take giant military shears to it, snap! bitten off in an instant; and nothing left in my hands but spools of khaki which could weave only a plain, flat, khaki design, however twisted they might be.

Not that it would be a good life. The war would be deadly all right. But I was used to finding something deadly lurking in anything I wanted, anything I loved. And if it wasn't there as for example with Phineas, then I put it there myself.

But there is more goodness in Gene than he knows. Phineas, in his need, gives Gene the opportunity to do good and unknowingly gives Gene the self-confidence to be free once more. For Gene's act had damaged Phineas' athletic excellence and, worse, threatened the basis for Phineas' humanity; and Phineas uses his remaining strength to deny this loss. He proceeds to recreate his world through Gene's friendship and athletic development. In this experience, Gene, freed now of envy and despair, understands himself and Phineas.

GENE'S REDEMPTION

In fulfilling this second gift of freedom Gene achieves a tragic victory. He is the only one in the book to know himself. The demands on his capacity are symbolized by the workout during which Gene escapes old limits to a new and comfortable level of achievement.

After making two circuits of the walk every trace of energy was as usual completely used up, and as I drove myself on all my scattered aches found their usual way to a profound seat of pain in my side. My lungs as usual were fed up with all this work and from now on would only go rackingly through the motions. My knees were boneless again, ready at any minute to let my lower legs telescope up into the thighs. My head felt as though different sections of the cranium were grinding into each other.

Then, for no reason at all, I felt magnificent. It was as though the aches and exhaustion were all imagined, created from nothing in order to keep me from truly exerting myself. Now my body seemed at last to say, "Well, if you must have it, here!" and an accession of strength came flooding through me. Buoyed up, I forgot my usual feeling of routine self-pity when working out, I lost myself, oppressed mind along with aching body; all entanglements were shed, I broke into the clear.

After the fourth circuit, like sitting in a chair, I pulled up in front of Phineas.

"You're not even winded," he said.
"I know."
"You found your rhythm, didn't you, that third time around. Just as you came into that straight part there."
"Yes, right there."
"You've been pretty lazy all along, haven't you?"
"Yes, I guess I have been."
"You didn't even know anything about yourself."

It is Gene, the scholar, who understands that his sin against Phineas was due to an ignorance of his own nature and that war is a manifestation of a general defensive ignorance in mankind. John K. Crabbe wrote,

In a moment reminiscent of the shooting of the Arab in Camus' *The Stranger*, Gene cripples his friend and sets in motion a chain of events which leads with Hellenic inevitability to Phineas' death.

But unlike the hero of *The Stranger*, Gene redeems his guilt with understanding. So, at the end of the book, Gene more than Phineas embodies the Greek ideal. He has arete; he has unity. Gene has penetrated the appearances which deceive others and made a harmony of his own that is more profound and more stable than Phineas'.

As pain that cannot forget falls drop by drop upon the heart and in our despite, against our will, comes wisdom to us from the awful grace of God.

Aeschylus

CHAPTER 4

Characterization in *A Separate Peace*

Finny as Villain

Joseph E. Devine

Since the publication of *A Separate Peace*, many critics have likened the character Finny to the Greek
ideals of beauty, strength, athleticism, and respect
for the individual. Joseph E. Devine finds such comparisons wholly misguided and instead offers a
scathing critique of Finny's character. In his interpretation, Devine concludes that Knowles implicitly
uses Finny to symbolize a deceitful, psychotic, Nazi-
like enemy to Western democracy. In contrast to the
villain-like Finny, Gene represents a respectable, patriotic, all-American boy. Devine taught English at
West Seattle High School in Washington.

John Knowles' *A Separate Peace*, a very popular novel
among high school students, has generally been accepted as
a story about youth and war at an Eastern prep school.
Phineas (Finny), one of the two central characters, is characterized as a happy, self-confident, pleasantly eccentric
youth who excels in athletics. Gene, his best friend, comes
off as a scholarly boy whose attitudes towards Phineas are
darkly ambivalent.

FINNY'S PERFIDY

Nothing could be further from the truth. Careful study reveals that Phineas is in reality the villain—and much more
to boot. There are many clues to Finny's perfidy but the most
obvious one comes in the Winter Carnival scene. One of the
prizes offered in the athletic competition is a copy of the *Iliad*. This great classic, along with many other prizes, some
nonsensical, some even vulgar, was donated by Finny. His
donation of this particular book represents his rejection of
the Greek contributions to Western culture. Here for the first
time we get a glimpse of Finny's intrinsic aversion to art,
beauty, justice, order, freedom, and democracy. We see

From Joseph E. Devine, "The Truth About *A Separate Peace*," *English Journal*, vol. 58,
no. 4 (April 1969), pp. 519–20. Copyright 1969 by the National Council of Teachers of
English. Reprinted with permission.

clearly that these concepts, which encompass the well-springs of Western democracy, are repugnant to Finny's inner beliefs.

Finny's rejection of democracy, the essence of the American political system, explains perfectly his feigned rejection of the existence of the war. How diabolical is his scheme! For if there is no war, then freedom is not being defended. And if freedom goes unprotected then the world will surely fall to the tender mercies of one Adolf Hitler, dictator of Nazi Germany. Finny's insistence that there is no war lulls the students of Devon into believing that there really is no war. And these boys are soon to be drafted into the Army! What a shock it will be when they find out that they are now soldiers in that war! That this shock would have a deleterious effect on their fighting potential is part of Finny's scheme. The case of Elwin "Leper" Lepellier, who cracks up from Army life, I think, leaves no doubt as to the truth of this thesis.

The implication drawn from the aforementioned facts that Finny is a German agent is *not* coincidental. His motivation is clear: he is bitter about having been "jounced" out of a tree by Gene Forrester, his best friend. Gene shoulders the blame manfully, even confessing that he was the cause of the accident. Even that, apparently does not assuage Finny.

Additional proof of Finny's guilt is provided by the writings above each line of text in the *Iliad*. Ostensibly these lines comprise translations from Greek into English. But how can we be sure that they do not conceal some code? When Brinker Hadley announces that the games are open, Finny interrupts him and *insists* on the presence of the "eternal flame." He then seizes the copy of the *Iliad*, sprinkles it with hard cider, and sets it ablaze. Surely this destruction by fire of a Greek classic, violated by the presence within its sacred pages of a furtive code, symbolizes the fiery Gotterdamerung of Western civilization. This act, of course, brings to mind the fearful Nazi book-burning rallies.

GENE AND FINNY: POLAR OPPOSITES

John Knowles, then, is not very subtly using Gene and Finny to symbolize, respectively democracy and totalitarianism. Finny, the German spy, is a deceitfully clever, decadent, psychosis-ridden Eastern rich kid. Gene, on the other hand, is a perfectly healthy, hard studying, all-American boy.

In spite of this evidence, some of the untrained minds who have attempted to analyze this book, have attacked Gene for "pushing" Finny out of the tree and have accused him of being jealous of Finny, an idler who spends most of his time on sports. These bleeding hearts fail to realize that Gene is an authentic war hero. Actually, Gene rendered a great service to his country by partially destroying the effectiveness of a dangerous spy. If this be so—and reason demands it—then Gene was doing no more than his duty. He was trying to protect his country, the highest form of patriotism.

Knowles further emphasizes these facts by the masterful use of implicit symbols and comparisons. Finny's very name indicates that there is something fishy. The word "Devon" itself is the name of a cow, distinguished by its red color, found in England. This pointed reference to the color red suggests a concealed Communist apparatus in rural England. Does not this hidden Red espionage ring abroad find its echo in the presence of a Nazi spy at Devon? The answer is an emphatic *yes.* The foregoing is an involuted analogy to be sure, but an obvious one to those who seek only the truth.

Probably the most remarkable phenomenon of all is that most teachers completely overlook many of these points when teaching this book. Many of them attach an entirely different interpretation to these facts. But this merely points out the great luxury of teaching English—one can be completely wrong, but nobody can prove it.

Finny as Greek God

Marvin E. Mengeling

In this selection, Marvin E. Mengeling argues that *A Separate Peace* is John Knowles's exploration of the mythic quest for Greek ideals. To this end, Knowles created Finny as a Greek god, much like Phoebus Apollo. The godlike Finny represents light and youth, although he deteriorates physically. Finny's subsequent death—and all gods must die physically—offers Gene salvation. Finny's lingering spiritual influence enables Gene to temper his envy and fear and thereby achieve maturity and self-knowledge. Mengeling was on the faculty of the English Department at Wisconsin State University in Oshkosh, Wisconsin.

A Separate Peace stands as a book of classic richness and meaning, one whose major worth as a work of art emanates from the subtle interaction of two chief levels of significance: the literal and the mythic. It is with the mythic level that I am most concerned. . . .

For John Knowles the mythic journey of *A Separate Peace* involves a paradoxical quest for the ideals of the Golden Age of Greece; paradoxical in that a step backward chronologically in a search for value becomes for man a step forward emotionally.

We are informed from numerous sources that the character of the so-called "golden" Greek consisted of energy and experimentation, but never unaccompanied by the tempering agents of clear judgment and good reason. They were a people of deep curiosity concerning the natural world in which they lived. Study of nature led almost inevitably to an appreciation of its balance and essential simplicity. The Greek concept of the ideal life, then, was grounded in achieving harmony between one's abilities and interests. One should strive for that healthy and happy equilibrium which exists between action and thought. All attempts would prove impotent, how-

Excerpted from Marvin E. Mengeling, "*A Separate Peace:* Meaning and Myth," *English Journal*, vol. 58, no. 9 (December 1969), pp. 1322–29. Copyright 1969 by the National Council of Teachers of English. Reprinted with permission. Notes and references in the original have been omitted in this reprint.

ever, if individual man did not avoid the dreaded *hubris*, that insolence and pride which separates man from his fellows and sets him at war with harmony. Truly, "man is the measure of all things," but only, to paraphrase Socrates, if man truly knows himself. Harmony and balance, far removed from the haunts of pride and insolence, are a portion of that humanism which Phineas offers Gene.

PHOEBUS APOLLO

Phineas, of course, depicts more than just a generalized approach to life, for in a deeper, more exact sense he portrays a god, called by some the most Greek of all the gods, Phoebus Apollo. Phoebus Apollo, god of light and youth—represented in art as handsome, young, athletic—was a beautiful, glowing figure. He was not only the master musician but also the Archer god. Most significantly, Phoebus Apollo was the healer, the god who first taught man the healing art, a specialist in purifications who taught correct procedures for avoiding evils, ills, superstitions, and fears. He was the god of light; in him there was no darkness, no falsehood, but only truth. Due to such brilliant attributes Phoebus Apollo was quite probably confused by the later Greeks with Helios, Greek god of the sun, and for this reason is also known as the sun god, shown in much later art with rays of light shooting from his head. This point is of no small importance when one recalls the many scenes in *A Separate Peace* in which Phineas is directly connected to the sun, and especially those scenes in which rays of sunlight seem to burst from the form of Phineas in silhouette.

EXORCISING FEAR

It was through the healthy creation of such deities as Phoebus Apollo that the Greek people somehow largely dismissed from their lives the most brutalizing of all human emotions—fear. A world which had been haunted for untold ages by dark and unknown terrors was somehow miraculously changed, in Greece at least, to a world with much beauty, reason, and common sense. It is from the black labyrinth of such a brutalizing emotion as fear that Phineas at last salvages Gene and starts him down the path to a humanistic loyalty, "beginning with him and me and radiating outward past the limits of humanity toward spirits and clouds and stars."

There is an obvious pattern of Greek allusions in *A Separate Peace*. At one important point Phineas is described as "Greek inspired and Olympian." He is athletic and beautiful, blazing with "sunburned health." He walks before Gene in a "continuous flowing balance" that acknowledges an "unemphatic unity of strength." Though Gene, as any boy his age, is often given to imaginative hyperbole (as we all are when our Gods are involved), there is no doubt that to him and the other boys Phineas is "unique." Behind his "controlled ease" there rests the "strength of five people." And even if he cannot carry a tune as well as he carries other people, Phineas loves all music, for in it, as in the sea and all nature, he seems to sense the basic beat of life, health, and regeneration. His voice carries a musical undertone. It is as naked and sincere as his emotions. Only Phineas has what to Gene is a "shocking self-acceptance." Only Phineas never really lies.

At the beginning of the book Phineas sets the stage for his own special function. On forcing Gene out of the tree for the first time, he says, "I'm good for you that way. You tend to back away otherwise." Phineas knows that Gene must jump from the tree, because in some cryptic fashion which only he seems to understand, they are "getting ready for the war." Among the Devon boys only Phineas knows that they must be conforming in every possible way to what is happening and what is going to happen in the general warfare of life. The first necessary step toward successful confrontation of what is going to happen rests in self-knowledge.

THE PHINEAS OUTLOOK

One cold winter morning, after Finny's "accident," Gene is running a large circle around Phineas, being trained, as Phineas puts it, for the 1944 Olympic Games. With his broken leg Phineas knows that the Games are closed to himself; he will have to participate through Gene, who was always as disinterested in sports as Phineas seemed to be in his studies. Gene is huffing, his body and lungs wracked with tiring pains that hit like knife thrusts. "Then," he says, "for no reason at all, I felt magnificent. It was as though my body until that instant had simply been lazy, as though the aches and exhaustion were all imagined, created from nothing in order to keep me from truly exerting myself. Now my body seemed at last to say, 'Well, if you must have it, here!' and an accession of strength came flooding through me. Buoyed up, I forgot my usual feeling of routine self-pity when working out, I lost myself, oppressed mind along with aching body; all entanglements were shed, I broke into the clear." After finishing the grueling run Gene and his Olympian coach have the following significant and two-leveled conversation:

> Phineas: You found your rhythm, didn't you, that third time around. Just as you came into that straight part there.
> Gene: Yes, right there.
> Phineas: You've been pretty lazy all along, haven't you?
> Gene: Yes, I guess I have been.
> Phineas: You didn't even know anything about yourself.
> Gene: I don't guess I did, in a way.

At one point Gene decides that Phineas' seemingly irrepressible mind (he ignored many of the small rules of behavior at Devon) was not completely unleashed, that he did abide by certain rules of conduct "cast in the form of Commandments." One rule is that you should not lie. Another is that one should always pray because there just might be a God. And there is the idea that is the key to the entire Phineas outlook: that "You always win at sports." To Phineas, sports were the absolute good, the measure of the balanced life. The significance that eludes Gene at this point, as it eludes most people everywhere today, is that everyone *can* and *should* win at sports, because in the Greek view of Phineas sports are not so much a competition against others—a matter of pride and winning at any cost—but a competition against oneself, a healthy struggle in which one measures his capacities without ego, fear, or *hubris.* We easily identify with Gene's total disbelief when Phineas privately shatters a school swimming record but wishes no public recognition. He says, "I just wanted to see if I could do it. Now I know." This is the Olympic Games spirit as it should be and as it perhaps once was. Phineas adds, "when they discovered the circle they created sports." And when they discovered the circle they also created the universal symbol for the whole man.

THE WINTER CARNIVAL

Using classical myth as a tool for understanding the present is hardly new to literature. James Joyce, for one, demonstrated with genius its relevance to modern life and art. In *A Separate Peace*, myth is molded and altered when necessary to fit Knowles' dramatic purposes. The episode concerning the Devon Winter Carnival, that special artistic creation of Phineas, not only provides excellent examples of Knowles' mythological method, but is thematically very important as marking the symbolic point of passage for the Olympic spirit—its flame of life—from Phineas to Gene. It is during the carnival scene that Phineas, leg in cast, dances a rapturous and wild bacchanal, his special, and last, "choreography of peace." For the briefest of moments in a drab world's drabbest season Phineas creates a world of Dionysian celebration that infuses Gene with divine enthusiasm. At this point, Knowles chooses to blend the figure of the young Phoebus Apollo (Phineas before the fall) with that of the resurrected Dionysus (Phineas after his fall; who has finally discovered what "suffering" is).

In ancient Greece the Dionysian festival began in the spring of the year with Greek women travelling into the hills to be "reborn" again through mystical union with the God of Wine. They danced, they drank, they leaped in wild frenzy as all restraint melted away. At the center of the ceremony they seized a goat, perhaps a bull, sometimes a man (all believed to be incarnations of Dionysus), and tore the live victim to shreds. A ceremony of pagan communion followed in which the victim's blood was quaffed and the flesh eaten, whereby the communicants thought their souls would be entered and possessed by their resurrected god. Knowles surely bore in mind the festival of Dionysus when erecting his superb carnival scene. In a sense, this invention of Phineas marks his resurrection, for it is the first project in which he has exhibited personal interest since his fall. At last, though briefly, the "old" Phineas seems to have returned somewhat in body and spirit. Amid a scene of mayhem, in which "there was going to be no government, even by whim," the boys circle around Brinker Hadley, throw themselves upon him, and forcibly take his jealously guarded cache of hard cider. They drink, they dance, they throw off the fear and "violence latent in the day," losing themselves completely in the festival of Phineas. Then, with the burning of Homer's book of war, *The Iliad*, a specialized version of the Olympic Games begins, a somewhat nicer type of "warfare." Soon, from the monarch's chair of black walnut—whose regal legs and arms end in the paws and heads of lions—Phineas rises to full height on the prize table, and at the "hub" of the proceedings begins his wild bacchanal. Gene says that "Under the influence not I know of the hardest cider but of his own inner joy at life for a moment as it should be, as it was meant to be in his nature, Phineas recaptured that magic gift for existing primarily in space, one foot conceding briefly to gravity its rights before spinning him off again into the air. It was his wildest demonstration of himself, of himself in the kind of world he loved; it was his choreography of peace."

Prior to the Carnival, Gene says he had acted simply as a "Chorus" to Phineas, but now the beautiful boy-god, sitting amid the tabled prizes, makes a request of Gene: on a physical level, to qualify for their Olympic Games; on a spiritual level, to qualify for salvation. During the past weeks Gene has made the Phineas outlook and spirit more and more a part of his own, and so infused, he now reacts to the request in the only way possible: ". . . it wasn't cider which made me in this moment champion of everything he ordered, to run as though I were the abstraction of speed, to walk the half-circle of statues on my hands, to balance on my head on top of the icebox on top of the Prize Table, to jump if he had asked it across the Naguamsett and land crashing in the middle of Quackenbush's boat house, to accept at the end of it amid a clatter of applause—for this day even the schoolboy egotism of Devon was conjured away—a wreath made from the evergreen trees which Phineas placed on my head."

GENE'S GROWTH

Somehow, Gene has mystically been passed the saving spirit and code of Phineas. His new growth and knowledge are immediately tested. The Carnival ends prematurely when Gene receives an ominous telegram from Leper Lepellier asking Gene to come to his winterbound home in Vermont. Gene suspects that the fruits of such an isolated meeting will not be pleasant ones, but he also knows that he must sometimes face certain harsh realities alone, even if only a little at a time. Also, he realizes that he has a chance to endure now, for the influence of Phineas, god of sun, light, and truth, is always with him. As he finally approaches Leper's house he thinks that, like Phineas, "The sun was the blessing of the morning, the one celebrating element, an aesthete with no purpose except to shed radiance. Everything else was sharp and hard, but this *Grecian sun* (my italics) evoked joy from every angularity and blurred with brightness the stiff face of the countryside. As I walked briskly out the road the wind knifed at my face, but this sun caressed the back of my neck."

Now Gene does not immediately dash away when learning the grim tale of Leper's Section-Eight. The summer before Gene would have run quickly from such unpleasantness back to the maternal and more secure confines of old Devon, but now he needs "too much to know the facts," and though he finally does run away in the "failing sunshine" from the horrible details of Leper's casualty, he has shown strong signs of significant progress. "I had had many new experiences," Gene says, "and I was growing up."

THE DEATH OF PHINEAS

Physically, Phineas dies. The reasons are twofold. All gods must die physically; it is in their nature to be spiritual, and in the case of many, sacrificial. Phineas dies that Gene might live. Second, Phineas must be crushed physically to emphasize that the present world is really no place for the full-blown powers and principles which he represents in his symbolic guise of Phoebus Apollo. Changes in man's psychological makeup do not erupt like some overnight volcano of the sea. Such transition is always painfully slow, necessarily too slow. But perhaps now, in a ruptured world that is heaped with war's unromantic statistics and computerized cruelties, humanity will choose to reemerge from its emotional rubble. Gene always had the brilliance, the IQ, the "brains," but they were untempered by a proper emotional stance. He had envy and he had great fear. He had no balance. Phineas disappears in a physical sense, but his spiritual influence, a portion of his code, will endure in Gene—a tiny spark in the darkness searching for human tinder. The spirit of Apollo has possessed its prophet and will now speak through his mouth. Gene's self has become "Phineas-filled," and to Gene, Phineas was "present in every moment of every day" since he died. First Gene and then perhaps a few others will relearn the road to Greece. "I was ready for the war," Gene says, "now that I no longer had any hatred to contribute to it. My fury was gone, I felt it gone, dried up at the source, withered and lifeless. Phineas had absorbed it and taken it with him, and I was rid of it forever." Even fifteen years later when Gene returns to Devon he approaches the school down a street lined with houses to him reminiscent of "Greek Revival temples." The cause of wars within and without the individual, that "something ignorant in the human heart," has now been exorcised.

THE MARK OF THE GREEK SPIRIT

The purgated emotions of negative content had been fear, jealousy, and hate, emotions which result in wars both personal and global. The positive emotions which then must replace them are friendship, loyalty, and love toward all mankind and nature, emotions which result in peace and an appreciation of life and its beauty. Even though Phineas had broken every minor and stuffy Devon regulation, never had a student seemed to love the school more "truly and deeply." Edith Hamilton writes in *The Greek Way* that "To rejoice in life, to find the world beautiful and delightful to live in, was a mark of the Greek spirit which distinguished it from all that had gone before. It is a vital distinction." So although the world is not yet ready for the apotheosis of some golden Greek Apollo, perhaps it is prepared, after its most recent blood gluts and promises of human extinction, for the first faltering step toward a world full of the Phineas-filled, a step which must necessarily begin with the conquering of a small part of the forest of self—a step toward the far frontiers of ancient Greece.

The Adult Image

Sister M. Amanda Ely

A Separate Peace depicts adults who are described as
fat, old, gassy, and inane. In the following essay, Sister
M. Amanda Ely traces Knowles's treatment of each
adult character, concluding that all adults in the book
are lacking. Because Knowles depicts the adults as inadequate, intolerant and ineffectual, *A Separate Peace*
is bereft of any suitable adult role models. Ely was the
Chairman of the English Department of Trinity High
School in River Forest, Illinois, when she wrote this
essay for the *English Journal.*

It is a commonplace that Dad comes out something less than
a winner in television drama of modern life. An examination
of the adult in . . . *A Separate Peace* discloses some of the same
inadequacies and reveals interesting contrasts in the adult image and in the adolescent-adult relationship. . . .

Gene Forrester, the narrator of the book, and his best
friend Finny attend a summer session at Devon as sixteen-
year-olds, too young to enlist in World War II. Because they
"remind the schoolmasters of peace," they enjoy a certain
indulgence even during the following winter session that the
older boys are denied.

In this novel, adults are out of touch, out of contact with the
adolescent. Much of this amorphism is explained by the fact
that the theme of the novel concerns the maturation of the
teens because of interrelations with their peers and the fact
that the boys are away from parental direction. No parent of either major character, Gene or Finny, appears or is named in
the book. Gene comes from the South, Finny from Boston. That
is the substance of family background given. The adults of *A
Separate Peace* are school officials, doctors, or parents of minor characters. There is no real problem of rebellion against
authority, although the difference in Gene's and Finny's attitudes toward authority is one of the major character contrasts.

Excerpted from Sister M. Amanda Ely, "The Adult Image in Three Novels of Adolescent Life," *English Journal*, vol. 56, no. 8 (November 1967), pp. 1127–31. Copyright
1967 by the National Council of Teachers of English. Reprinted with permission.

During the idyllic summer term, the school authorities are extremely tolerant, enforcing "such rules as they knew; missing dinner was one of them." During the summer the headmasters "modified their usual attitude of floating, chronic disapproval." During winter, Gene tells the reader, they regarded anything unexpected in a student with suspicion; "anything we said or did was potentially illegal." In June they uncoiled, believed the students with them half of the time, and that the students spent the other half trying to make fools of them. Upon detecting this streak of tolerance, Finny decided "that they [the adults] were beginning to show commendable signs of maturity."

THE ADULT-ADOLESCENT RELATIONSHIP

Finny and Gene attend a tea at the headmaster, Mr. Patch-Withers' house, where Mrs. Patch-Withers trembles at every cup tinkle and talks of the importance of the Americans being careful of works of art in their bombing of Europe. Gene and Finny try hard not to sound as inane in their conversation with the masters and their wives as the adults sound to them.

Besides the schoolmasters, there is the school chaplain, Mr. Carhart, who has an unreal view of the war and who is much moved at his own sermon on God in the foxholes.

The doctors and nurses who treat Finny are characterized by their verbosity. The nurse is Miss Windbag, RN; Doctor Stanpole has a vocabulary so large—"probably a million words"—that Gene reasons he has to use it up before he can start over again.

Though the reader senses the doctor's sympathy for Gene in his agony over Finny's suffering and death, the doctor despite his prolixity is never able to communicate his comparison to the boy.

Though the parents of the leading characters do not materialize, two parents do appear, both in an unfavorable role. Leper's mother is a willy-nilly woman who distrusts Gene at first because of his rowdiness but who is later reconciled because he likes her cooking. Mr. Hadley, Brinker's father, a distinguished white-haired man with a healthy pink face, has an idealistic, romantic view of the war that the boys consider completely unrealistic. He makes patriotic gestures and ennobling speeches about their opportunity to serve their country as frogmen. "I'd give anything to be a kid again," he says. The boys have short patience with his "people will get to respect you for your war memories." Gene decides that accepting a friend's shortcomings includes his parents, even "his Nathan Hale attitude."

Finny also adopts an unrealistic attitude about the war, but of a different ilk. He claims the war is made up by "the fat old men" who don't want the younger generation crowding them out of their jobs. There is no food shortage, explains Finny: "The fat old men had all the steaks delivered to their clubs where they are getting fatter."

MEANINGFUL NAMES

The names of the adults in *A Separate Peace* speak their characters: Mr. Prud'homme, Mr. Patch-Withers, Doctor Stanpole, Miss Windbag, Mr. Pike, Mr. Ludsbury. The most frequently used adjectives describing adults are fat, old, fragile, tolerant, indulgent, gassy, inane; their faces are most often pink or turning red.

No adult in the book is a suitable model for a teen: there is no communication between boy and adult that seems natural or normal. The adults are either being spoofed by Finny's cleverness, looking the other way during the idyllic summer term, or being rather ineffectual in their efforts at discipline during the more regulated winter term. The boys don't take the adults seriously under any circumstances.

CHRONOLOGY

1926

John Knowles is born September 16 in Fairmont, West Virginia.

1939–1945

World War II begins in Europe; United States enters war in 1941 after Japanese attack on Pearl Harbor.

1942

Knowles enters Phillips Exeter Academy, a preparatory school in New Hampshire.

1943

Attends Exeter's Anticipatory Program, a wartime academic session that runs from June to September; belongs to a group called the Suicide Society, whose members jump from a tree into a river.

1944–1945

Graduates from Phillips Exeter Academy; enters Yale in the fall; joins the air force and is assigned to the aviation cadet program; World War II ends; discharged from the air force in November, 1945.

1946–1949

Attends Yale; earns bachelor's degree in English.

1950-1952

Works as a reporter for the *Hartford Courant.*

1953

"A Turn in the Sun," Knowles's first story, is published in *Story* magazine.

1954

Begins writing *A Separate Peace.*

1956

Cosmopolitan publishes the short story "Phineas"; accepts a position as associate editor for *Holiday* magazine in Philadelphia.

1959

A Separate Peace is published by Secker and Warbury in Britain; receives favorable reviews.

1960

A Separate Peace is published in America by Macmillan on February 29; wins Rosenthal Award from the National Institute of Arts and Letters and the William Faulkner Award; is nominated for the National Book Award; Knowles leaves *Holiday* so that he can devote himself to writing and travel; travels to Syria, Lebanon, and other countries abroad, gathering impressions that will appear in *Double Vision: American Thoughts Abroad.*

1962

Publishes *Morning in Antibes*, which receives negative reviews.

1964

Publishes *Double Vision: American Thoughts Abroad*, a collection of essays.

1966

Publishes *Indian Summer.*

1968

Publishes *Phineas: Six Stories*, a collection of short stories.

1971

Publishes novel *The Paragon.*

1972

Hollywood releases movie version of *A Separate Peace.*

1974

Publishes novel *Spreading Fires.*

1978

A Vein of Riches, a historical novel, is published.

1981

Peace Breaks Out, a sequel to *A Separate Peace,* is published.

1986

Publishes *The Private Life of Axie Reed.*

FOR FURTHER RESEARCH

ABOUT *A SEPARATE PEACE*

Douglas Alley, "Teaching Emerson Through *A Separate Peace*," *English Journal*, January 1981.

Hallman B. Bryant, A Separate Peace: *The War Within*. Boston: Twayne, 1990.

———, "Finny's Pink Shirt," *Notes on Contemporary Literature*, 1984.

John K. Crabbe, "On the Playing Fields of Devon," *English Journal*, 1963.

Linda Haniz and Roy Huss, "*A Separate Peace:* Filming the War Within," *Literature Film Quarterly*, 1975.

John Knowles, "My Separate Peace," *Esquire*, March 1985.

Regina Pomeranz, "Self-Betrayal in Modern American Fiction," *English Record*, April 1964.

Claire Rosenfield, "The Shadow Within: The Conscious and Unconscious Use of the Double," *Daedalus: Journal of the American Academy of Arts and Sciences*, 1963.

Mildred Travis, "Mirror Images in *A Separate Peace* and *Cat and Mouse*," *Notes on Contemporary Literature*, 1975.

Hayden Ward, "The Arnoldian Situation in *A Separate Peace*," *Bulletin of West Virginia Association of College English*, 1974.

HISTORICAL AND LITERARY BACKGROUND

Richard Chase, *The American Novel and Its Tradition*. Garden City, NY: Doubleday, 1957.

H.D. Curran, "The Summer Session of 1942," *Phillips Exeter Academy Bulletin*, 1942.

Howard Easton, "Life in the Forties," *Exonian*, October 28, 1972.

Chester E. Eisinger, *The 1940s: Profile of a Nation in Crisis*. Garden City, NY: Anchor Books, 1969.

Henry C. Herge et al., *Wartime College Training Programs of the Armed Services.* Washington, DC: American Council on Education, 1948.

George-Michael Sarotte, *Like a Brother, Like a Lover.* Garden City, NY: Doubleday, 1978.

Willey Lee Umphlett, *The Sporting Myth and the American Experience: Studies in Contemporary American Fiction.* Lewisburg, PA: Bucknell University Press, 1975.

Myron R. Williams, *The Story of Phillips Exeter Academy.* Exeter, NH: Exeter, 1957.

H.P. Willmott, *The Great Crusade: A New Complete History of the Second World War.* New York: Viking Penguin, 1989.

Works by John Knowles

A Separate Peace (1959)
Morning in Antibes (1962)
Double Vision: American Thoughts Abroad (1964)
Indian Summer (1966)
Phineas: Six Stories (1968)
The Paragon (1971)
Spreading Fires (1974)
A Vein of Riches (1978)
Peace Breaks Out (1981)
A Stolen Past (1983)
The Private Life of Axie Reed (1986)

INDEX